SUPERPOWERS UNLEASHED!

Identify and Monetize Your Senses

Tammy De Mirza

ALCHEMY
PUBLISHING, LLC.

Copyright © 2024 Tammy De Mirza

All rights reserved. No part of this book may be used, reproduced, distributed, or transmitted in any form or by any means, including photocopying, recording, taping, or by graphic, electronic, or mechanical methods, without the prior written permission of the author, except in the case of brief quotations embodied in critical reviews and certain other noncommercial uses permitted by copyright law.

Because of the dynamic nature of the Internet, any web addresses or links contained in this book may have been changed since publication and may no longer be valid. The words expressed in this work are solely those of the author and do not necessarily reflect the views of the publisher, and the publisher hereby disclaims any responsibility for them.

The author of this book does not dispense medical advice or prescribe the use of any technique as a form of treatment for physical, emotional, or medical problems without the advice of a physician, either directly or indirectly. The intent of the author is only to offer information of a general nature to help you in your quest for emotional and spiritual well-being. In the event you use any of the information in this book for yourself, which is your constitutional right, the author and the publisher assume no responsibility for your actions.

Disclaimer: The information contained in this book is for educational and informational purposes only and is not intended as a substitute for professional advice. The author and publisher assume no responsibility or liability for any errors or omissions in the content of this book. The advice and strategies contained herein may not be suitable for your situation. You should consult with a professional where appropriate. The author and publisher deny any liability for any loss, damage, or disruption caused by the use or misuse of this book. Any perceived slight of specific people or organizations is unintentional.

Library of Congress Cataloging-in-Publication Data

ISBN: 979-8-9865084-2-9
ISBN: 979-8-9865084-3-6
ISBN: 979-8-9865084-4-3

NOTES & INTENTIONS:

DEDICATION

To my beautiful grands - Grae, Finn, Eden, Ryder, Evie, and Milo,

You are amazing souls that I am privileged to share this life with! May you benefit from the content in this book by truly knowing who you are, understanding how you benefit the world, and using this knowledge to catapult your success in all areas.

Thank you for being such an integral part of my world, for loving me unconditionally, and for teaching me so much. You make my life incredibly special, and I love you so much!!!

With love - Gammy

PRAISE FOR SUPERPOWERS UNLEASHED!

"Superb ... Superpowers Unleashed is a life-changing book that empowers readers by helping them discover their unique abilities both personally and professionally. Tammy De Mirza writes like a dream as a coach and storyteller with vast experiential wisdom and will keep you thinking and rethinking about the transformative journey of self-discovery long after you've finished it. Read this book to move beyond the limits of the known and into an extraordinary new life. I recommend this book to everyone who wants to discover the phenomenal nature of consciousness, healing, and manifestation."

Deborah Giles – Founder and CEO of Center for Technology

"This book is a masterful piece of writing that the world has needed for a very long time - especially in today's age. I am so excited that Tammy has laid out a detailed portion of her knowledge about the Clairs in such a tangible way! From working with her personally, I can explicitly state that this wonderful, brave, and loving being has a wealth of knowledge that will change the world if people choose to take it in. This book is just one example of that.

I love that these concepts are taught by unifying the physical and metaphysical realms. She does this by explaining the spiritual nature of the Clairs (through her clients' and her own experiences), as well as grounding that information in the physical realm by giving everyone real-world examples of historical figures who displayed each one. She even goes as far as to give potential careers that each Clair would be helpful in. I don't know if the Clairs have ever been presented in the way that Tammy does, but I'm awfully glad this book exists!"

James Hayes- Norfolk, VA

"Unleashing Your Superpowers" by Tammy De Mirza is a must-read for anyone interested in exploring and enhancing their innate supernatural abilities through their 'Clair-senses'. This book offers a comprehensive guide to understanding and developing these senses to enhance various aspects of one's life, including personal relationships and career.

Personally, having worked with Tammy De Mirza, I've undergone a profound transformation, evolving into a more refined version of myself. With her adept insight and intuitive abilities, Tammy illuminates the world through a new lens, revealing truths obscured by our own limitations. Her approach is both transcendent and tailored, harmonizing universal principles with individual needs seamlessly. Empowering us with the knowledge that every moment presents a choice, she imparts the wisdom to embrace our power while carving the path toward fulfillment. She's not only saved me from my life-long depression and despair but also awakened me to the boundless possibilities of joy existing within our reality.

I rate "Unleashing Your Superpowers" 5 out of 5 stars for its ability to be both educational and transformative. It is especially valuable for those looking to identify and enhance their dominant Clair-sense to improve their quality of life. Whether you are a novice or someone already familiar with psychic phenomena, this book has something to offer. Use this guide to discover and develop your top Clair-sense, and watch as it positively transforms your approach to life's challenges and opportunities, strongly consider working with Tammy—it could change your life for the better.

Dr. Jeannie May – Nashville, TN

"Superpowers Unleashed isn't just a book; it's a catalyst for profound change, empowering readers to tap into their innate abilities and engage with the world through all five senses. Tammy De Mirza's eloquent writing and insightful guidance lead you on a journey of self-discovery that reshapes your perception of life. Her personal stories effortlessly connect, offering profound knowledge about your strengths and how to use them to navigate the world. This book has revolutionized my communication skills by uncovering my top Clairs and guiding me to develop them further. If you're ready to uncover your true self and navigate life with confidence, I wholeheartedly recommend immersing yourself in this transformative book."

Maria Lopez – Greenville, SC

Working with Tammy has transformed every relationship in my life, including my relationship with myself, my self-worth, and my finances. For the last 4 years, she has been an incredible catalyst for growth, transforming my life from inside out, time and time again. Not only does Tammy use her remarkable gifts to uncover the root causes of your challenges and help you heal from within, but she also empowers and teaches you to do the inner work yourself. If you're on a journey of personal growth and struggling to find someone who truly understands you, Tammy is the person you need.

While Tammy's work with each client is nothing short of extraordinary, her latest book, *Superpowers Unleashed! Identify and Monetize Your Senses*, is equally magnificent. This book offers the most insightful information on Clairs that I have ever encountered, whether in print or on YouTube. It reveals one of life's greatest gifts: understanding how you are constantly receiving guidance from God/Universe/Spirit.

Tammy is truly the Queen of Transformation and such a gift to this world. It has been an honor to work and learn from her.

Sveta Cross – Eagle River, AK

TESTIMONIALS

What Tammy's clients want you to know about working with her...

"Tammy is a spiritual guide, teacher, and mentor but titles don't do it justice! I won't attempt to articulate the intuitive abilities and spiritual basis and connection behind what she does but here are some things I know Tammy does really well...

- Creates a safe environment for you to heal, be seen, feel heard and accepted
- Shares her experiences and spiritual understandings in an applicable way to encourage self-experimentation and empowerment
- Helps you to know yourself, your needs, and your desires more intimately
- Intuitively communicates deeper-level thoughts and concepts that can offer opportunities to heal what was once unseen, unexplored, or simply unconscious

- Personalizes and grounds spiritual concepts into day-to-day life and makes a clear connection between spirit mind and body
- Challenges you to grow and elevate your consciousness and mindset while honoring your choice to remain right where you are
- Brings like-hearted souls into the community to support in their expansion and experiences"

Auti – Santa Barbara, CA

"An Intuitive, Life Coach and Mentor all rolled in one".

Shaun – Bridgewater, NJ

"I often describe Tammy as one of the most evolved souls on the planet with the ability to communicate with your soul and help you integrate that which you learn or transcend that which no longer serves you.

I also use phrases like:

- She is like 15 years of therapy on steroids but with actual healing, results, and integration.
- She is a master and leader to the leaders.

- Tammy is an enlightened human who has the ability to help you make quantum leaps by connecting you to yourself.
- A soul whisperer.
- One of the most beautiful souls on the planet who is here to fast-track a soul's knowing and intentional life.
- I could keep going...

You guys can probably tell why I have done so many life transformations. Each time, I learn something new about this lady".

Janet – Austin, TX

"In my limited experience with Tammy, all I can say is that she speaks the truth that feels like a lightning bolt to the heart. Simple truths that you've heard all your life but somehow, she brings it home powerfully so that you can't forget it. She has an undeniably impactful presence that feels so powerfully loving".

Ashley – Salt Lake City, UT

"I'm new to my experience with Tammy but so far, I would say she brings a calmness and understanding to your spirit. Not so that you understand her, but so that you can hear and understand yourself".

Laney – Austin, TX

"Tammy is a life coach, therapist, teacher, and friend rolled into one amazing lady. She intuitively guides you to unpack the BS stories that have been driving you and then asks you to consciously choose who your new you is!! The transformations happen as fast and as often as you are willing to move!!"

Sandie – Austin, TX

"Tammy is one of the most evolved souls on this planet that helps you breakthrough your trauma for you to do the inner work necessary to set yourself free.

She helps get the clarity you need as to why you are living small and feel stuck.

Tammy helps people to become aware and conscious so that with that awareness, they can begin to heal and live deeply meaningful, integrated, and empowered lives.

She helps people to see the truth of themselves, and teaches you how to transform your emotional, mental, and physical pain into love".

Maria – Greenville, SC

"Therapy on steroids! We spend our lives growing, evolving, learning. Why not do it faster on the soul-to-soul level".

Malena – Austin, TX

"I was once depressed and lost, struggling with grief, a special needs child, and a failing marriage. Desperately seeking change, a friend introduced me to Tammy, which started my transformation.

Tammy helped me understand myself, recognize my behavioral patterns, and realize how my thoughts shape my reality. She guided me to see my true self and choose better paths. With her assistance, I've discovered my gifts, gained a greater sense of who I authentically am, and learned to love myself. Despite ongoing challenges, I've managed to change my thinking, making life much more enjoyable. She has helped me free myself from my self-imposed prisons. She expertly identifies where you are and shows you how to help yourself reach your full potential. I highly recommend working with Tammy for anyone seeking life change".

Shirley – Pottstown, PA

"Working with Tammy has changed my life. The love that radiates from being with her provides such a safe space for growth and healing. One of the biggest impacts that she has had all my life is holding me accountable.

With Tammy's guidance and support, I now have the mindset that I live in a world that is happening for me, not to me.

She has such an incredible ability to see the authentic version of who you truly are. An amazing side effect of that is that when you make the changes, they stay. Years of traditional self-help have paled in comparison to my growth with Tammy. I will forever be grateful".

Courbyn – Austin, TX

Superpowers Unleashed!

PERSONAL NOTE TO YOU...

Hello Beautiful Souls!

I wrote this book for you so that you could see the superpowers waiting within you to be discovered, uncovered, and wielded. You are a singular wonder in your universe, and everything offered here is for you.

Let me share a little bit about my own life as you explore yours within these pages. Growing up, I felt different and alone because I didn't understand my experiences. I didn't have others around me to share these things with or to comprehend them, much less spectacularly use them to honor what was in alignment and what wasn't. I tried to be normal and to fit in. I innocently went about the world, acting as if others knew better than I did, and followed what they thought, said, or wanted. This left me disheartened, wanting to give up on life, and not thriving. I didn't feel seen, heard, or respected and my life became about being of service to others, instead of using my discernment to make decisions.

Many takers came into my life to take what I didn't own as mine. They seemed to know best, but I was left out, discouraged, and knew I had to make a change. I began to realize that unless I truly discovered who I was, and how I functioned and stopped fighting it, I would continue the path of mediocrity and hoping for change, but not experiencing it. I had to be the change!

That is why I wrote this book—to show you that you are not alone. You are beautifully and wonderfully made, and you have within you the ability to thrive in all things. Self-discovery is the key. Some of us thirst for more, to uncover hidden truths within us. We aren't satisfied with the mundane or what is perceived as normal. We have an innate knowing that we are more than our experiences, and there are deeper things to discover along the journey. We want more, and we always strive for more.

Through trial and error of not using my senses to discern my intuition consistently, discovering and uncovering it, and learning to use it for my good, I have found a beautiful secret. All of us possess fascinating, usable, and intimate sensory abilities that I call superpowers. Within these pages, you will discover the beauty of you. Understanding who you are, who you came here to be, and what you have to offer the world is the most important knowledge you can attain. There is only one of you! Besides everyone else is taken!

This book is an exploration of revealing your intuition and discernment, designed to help you gain confidence in knowing what to do and when to do it. You will learn to read your powerfully designed inner guidance system by understanding how you communicate with the world both on the physical and nonphysical levels. This will benefit not only you but will also be a catalyst for you to engage, connect, and be more intimate with the people in your life. By studying your abilities—your superpowers—you will be able to offer more than you ever dreamed possible.

Enjoy this journey of self-discovery. Know that you are not alone. My heart desires to help you connect to your intelligent inner guidance system, alleviate the pain of not getting what you want, and learn how to communicate in ways that catapult your success in relationships, and career, and manifest abundance in all areas of life.

YOU are a powerful being who has come here to experience the unlimited. This book offers you a way to understand yourself, to be authentic, and to know what is in alignment and what isn't, so you can make decisions based on your innate knowing.

This is a love offering, a compilation of my entire life studying human behavior and the predicaments we face. I have learned these things to help me navigate this world, and now, I share them with you to help you on your journey.

With all my love and best wishes on your discovery of YOU,

Jammy

CONTENTS

Foreword 1
Introduction 4
Chapter 1: Clair-Senses 18
   A Journey to Self-Mastery
Chapter 2: Clairvoyance 35
   Beyond Sight
Chapter 3: Embracing Clairaudience 79
   The Symphony Of The Unheard
Chapter 4: The Flavor Of Insight 118
   Unlocking The Power of Clairgustance
Chapter 5: Whispers Of The Invisible 158
   Mastering The Essence of Clairscent
Chapter 6: The Empathic Art 198
Chapter 7: Owning Your Genius 246
Acknowledgement 267
Free Resources 273
About The Author 275

FOREWORD

In "Superpowers Unleashed," Tammy De Mirza masterfully delves into the extraordinary capabilities that lie dormant within us all. This book is not merely about physical or fantastical abilities often portrayed in popular media but rather an exploration of the profound strengths and potentials inherent in the human spirit. From the depths of resilience that help us overcome life's greatest challenges to the boundless creativity that drives innovation and change, De Mirza illuminates the superpowers we each possess and can cultivate to transform our lives and the world around us. Tammy has the ability to see things in people that otherwise never get uncovered.

When I met the "Ultimate Intuitive" Tammy De Mirza, there was an immediate knowing of who she is, and what she does, and I saw her readiness to launch in a much bigger way. All she needed was a little encouragement, and our talks and time together, learning to accentuate her trade, helped her come out of hiding and own her genius. It has been a fun and rewarding experience to witness her journey. She has put her lifetime of accumulated wisdom into this new body of work, her book, "Superpowers Unleashed". Tammy comes from a heart of service and is 100% committed to making sure that anyone she works with will receive from her some of the greatest insights to move through blocks, tap into their own extraordinary gifts, and create outstanding results in a very short time. Tammy is one of the best in the world at what she does, if you have the opportunity to spend time or work with her, I highly recommend it!

Throughout this compelling journey, readers are invited to explore a diverse array of topics, each one shedding light on different facets of human potential. De Mirza examines the psychological underpinnings of resilience, the neuroscience of creativity, and the social dynamics that influence our ability to lead and inspire. She combines personal anecdotes, cutting-edge research, and practical exercises, providing a holistic approach to understanding and harnessing these superpowers. The book not only highlights the importance of self-awareness and continuous growth but also emphasizes the impact of these powers in fostering community and driving societal progress. Once you start reading, you will not be able to put the book down.

"Superpowers Unleashed" stands as a beacon of hope and empowerment, urging readers to look within and recognize the immense capabilities they hold. Tammy De Mirza's insightful narrative and actionable guidance offer a roadmap for unlocking our hidden strengths and achieving extraordinary outcomes. As you embark on this enlightening read, prepare to be inspired, challenged, and ultimately transformed, ready to unleash your superpowers and make an indelible mark on the world. Once again if you get the opportunity to work with her, you should definitely take advantage of that gift today!

Global Business Strategist - Bill Walsh

INTRODUCTION

Welcome to "Superpowers Unleashed! Identify and Monetize Your Senses." This book is a transformative guide designed to help you discover, understand, and leverage your unique sensory abilities—your superpowers—to create a more fulfilling and prosperous life. Whether you are seeking to improve and deepen your relationships, enhance your career, or simply unlock your full potential, this book provides the insights and tools you need.

I'll share a bit of my personal story, so you know how I began this self-exploration into my sensory superpowers. At the age of only 11 years old, I had an awakening experience that altered everything I knew, everything I thought and felt, and how I viewed the world. When I awoke the next morning, I knew before my eyes opened for the day, that I was not the same person. Overnight I went from being this little grammar school kid to someone who saw, heard, tasted, smelled, and felt things I'd never known before. My sensory abilities came alive as if I'd previously been in a coma.

I was in a state of shock because I realized that the experience I had the day before had somehow changed everything and I was rebirthed to a new way of being. I began to see things both physical and nonphysical, hear voices and thoughts of others, receive messages, and sense things that seemed beyond the wisdom of anyone that I'd met or spoken to. I could ask questions and receive clear and concise answers; even full explanations and downloads about a subject.

I began to read people's minds, and thoughts and knew what was transpiring in their lives without them speaking a word to me. I got into trouble at school, because I knew things about the kids I was in school with, and innocently thought that because I knew them, I could talk to them about it without an issue. To me, it was an easy thing to do, because I knew what was going on behind the scenes of the kids I was with.

An example of this was me going up to a kid and asking him why he didn't tell me that his grandmother was in the hospital for three days and almost died, because I would have prayed for her. He looked at me in shock and said "Tammy, why are you saying this? My grandmother isn't in the hospital!" That night, he went home and asked his parents and they got angry at me, because what I had said was the truth and they didn't want him to know, so they hid it from him. They wanted to know who I was and why I did this to them.

I began to experience pain and loneliness from this moment forward realizing that there may be an issue sometimes by expressing what I knew. The ramifications of sharing this were that he could no longer play with me on the playground, and I experienced the loss of him as a friend.

This one event started the pain of rejection that I felt and a bewildered way of living. I was confused, thought knowing things would be helpful to others, but was finding out that wasn't always the case. I was called a counselor in Jr. High and High School and my abilities developed with each passing year.

I begged my parents for two years to take me to Geer Memorial Baptist Church in Easley, South Carolina. I had been asking other kids where they went to church, and this seemed to be the happening place. We joined the church on my 13th birthday. I became deeply entrenched in the church and people were coming to me for all kinds of things. Some of them were health conditions, emotional trauma, as well as sharing private things with me that I had no idea how to cope with.

With time, I began to notice patterns and commonalities associated with what they were speaking with me about and what health conditions would correlate with their thoughts and stories. I started gathering a deeper understanding of life, how we think, and of the perceptions of events and how that started to dictate our behavior. I noticed that if God/Spirit wanted me to understand a certain experience, I would receive a repetition of multiple people coming to me with the same issue so that I could assimilate an entire study of what happened, the patterns they had developed because of their perception and belief of who they were and that once they were in a pattern of descent, they were not likely to change this pattern without some kind of intercession. People were finding me, and even though I felt obligated to help, didn't want them to know what I knew, and wanted to hide. I feared the strong reactions and consequences I was getting.

One day in my early 20's someone walked into my home, and I started to spontaneously scan them from their head to their toes. I read the energy and what was going on in their body, what the doctors had told them, and where the masses, cancer, and so many other things were specifically located in the body, along with the energy associated with it. I found myself with the intel of where their headaches formed, when they would start in the brain and where they spread, how often they had them, and specific details of what stressed them to the point of feeling the physical symptoms. I didn't know what to do with this information but knew inherently that if I put my hands on them and they wanted to be healed, they were healed. I watched cancer disappear and would tell them to please keep their appointments with their doctor and get the tests to prove that the masses/conditions had disappeared. I would ask each person not to share that I had helped them with anyone, for I was already growing weary of people finding me and didn't know how to process these miracles personally. People loved me and feared me at the same time because I wasn't normal. I began to feel like a freak of nature.

Once people had the symptoms of the predicaments disappear, they would come back to me with other predicaments/ailments and ask for more assistance, and the word spread, even though I didn't want to be known. I wanted to hide, conceal, and not feel what was transpiring, for I was way too young to know what to do with these abilities and I experienced both pain and pleasure at using them.

I began to assimilate information that correlated with specific subjects/things people had experienced in life and noticed that if God/Spirit wanted me to understand something more fully, I would suddenly get six to eight people with the same thing going on so that I could study it, read the energy of it, understand the human mind, how they processed it, and what information I could read and understand so that I would have the deeper perspective of how each person perceived their own his/herstory. I started to realize that everyone developed a different belief system because of the perception they associated with an event. This was shown to me with a different color, shape, symbol, vibration, sound, smell, taste, feeling, and a tapestry of woven threads they had in their lives through beliefs that had been adopted.

I could see the threads and know what colors they were and would pick one to pull out when a person came to me for help, and when I did, and explained to the person in front of me what happened in their lives and why they were experiencing what they were, the entire ball of threads would unravel and the power of the compounded issue, would disassemble and the human body would naturally heal. I was able to read the continued hamster wheel experiences, them running hard in life, trying to get a better life, but wasn't accomplishing it. I read their thoughts, beliefs, and the components that are involved in the five senses/Clairs and received a lot of information that was supernatural because I should not have known the details of what I was sharing. Nobody in their intimate lives did, so I shouldn't have either, but I did...

At an early age, a curiosity developed within me, of people who were very different from others, such as serial killers, and people who had spent time in prison. I read every book that I could about their human predicament, how it all started with them, and the levels of degradation experienced that would lead them to prostitution or other extreme behaviors. In studying these things, I began to realize that there were reciprocal patterns that developed, and once constituted, the inner GPS of someone was formed and once that was formed, it was very difficult for people to be able to free themselves from their self-imposed prisons. I started to be able to explain to people the patterns of their lives, seeing what had happened to them in the past, what decisions they made because of the inner pain they had experienced in their childhood, and how that was controlling their lives.

At the age of my late 20s, I was tired of helping so many others, I was losing sleep because people were calling me all hours of the night, people were showing up at my door, not saying what the reason was, as to why they were there, and I'd read their thoughts and explain it to them, and their inner healing began. I was exhausted and felt that I was not being given the time and energy to take care of my own children's needs and have spoken to them about that time in our lives when our front door, was a revolving scene of one person after another hearing about me and coming into our home. They have confirmed that they were confused, not understanding why so many people came so often wanting the attention of their mom.

Sometimes I would have my hand on the phone, knowing someone was about to call me and I'd answer immediately to their surprise, and say their name. Supernatural things were happening constantly and one evening, I was asked if I would help someone from another state, who was close to committing suicide, and I said, "Yes, I'll help her", I would be given the information about where she lived and how she would find me. The next day, about thirty minutes before she arrived, I was put on notice that she was lost in my neighborhood and would be at my home soon. I didn't see her physically pull into my driveway, but I saw her with Clairvoyance. I saw her turn right into my driveway with her dark blue Mercedes and where she parked. The structure of my home wasn't allowing me to see with my physical eyes, but I saw her clearly enough had my hand on the doorknob, and was waiting. When she tapped on the door, I immediately opened it and heard her say the very thing that I was told the night before, that she was lost in my neighborhood and needed help getting back to North Carolina where she lived. I told her that I'd been waiting for her since 8:30 pm the night before, for I knew she was coming to me. She didn't understand and was bewildered. I humored her and asked if I could show her something and she relented.

I stepped outside and asked her if she wanted directions, she wasn't supposed to be at my specific home, why did she come into a driveway with brick pillars and iron bars all around my front yard, when my neighbors were out on their porch having a great time and they were only about 20' from the road. She looked at me in recognition and I asked her if she wanted to come inside. As she crossed the threshold of my home, she exclaimed "I just decided an hour ago", and I finished the sentence for her, "That you are going to kill yourself, I was told this last night and you aren't going to, for you are here, so let's begin".

She cried and the inner healing work began. She left an entirely different person and I never heard from her again, but knew she was on a different path. She thanked me profusely and I went about my day with my kids.

Not long after this and so many other encounters, I began to be bewildered that some people were healed, but would come back with other ailments. I didn't fully comprehend the things I had studied about human behavior and mindset, but started to understand and see clearly that I was living in a painful personal environment and knew that I had to do my inner healing. One day, I shook my fist at God/Spirit and said that I wasn't mature enough to deal with the love-hate-relationship people had with me, because I seemed to be an instigator of truth and a lot of people didn't want that. Not only that, but I had my healing inner work to do and needed to get a divorce to begin a new life. I asked God/Spirit not to send me anyone else until I learned self-love, but that if I ever got to that point of maturity, to bring it back and I would once again be of service.

For thirteen years, I didn't mumble a prayer, didn't speak out loud to anyone about anything spiritual or religious. I was quiet, was remolding my life, and was overcoming attracting narcissistic behavior in others while focusing on my spiritual curriculum.

One day, after all those years and me being in a great place, buying my own home, and being independent, a friend of mine who owned a fabric store named Tony said he wanted to give me a book to read. As I touched the book days later, when I was back in his store, the energy of it came through my arms and suddenly I knew, "I was being activated again, and the calling was at my door to be of service again. I said 'Yes!"

As you can see, there was an evolution of my Clair-Senses, and with each step, I found myself wanting someone to talk to, someone to share this with, and certainly someone to guide me but could not find one. That is why I'm sharing this with you, so that you have someone who understands you, gets what you are going through, and can guide you to a level of maturation where the intangible becomes the tangible. Where the pain of being who you are becomes the resource of your discernment and wisdom and is used positively and productively in your everyday life.

I hope that from knowing more of my personal story you can now see that the sensory superpowers are innately within us all. That we use them most of the time haphazardly, but they are there, seeking opportunities to explore, develop, and be used in miraculous ways not only for ourselves but for others, for what is good for us, is good for everyone else.

Our senses—sight, hearing, taste, smell, and touch—are not just physical abilities but gateways to deeper intuitive insights. In "Superpowers Unleashed," we explore these senses through the lens of the five Clair-Senses: Clairvoyance, Clairaudience, Clairgustance, Clairscent, and Clairsentience. Each of these extrasensory perceptions offers a unique pathway to understanding the world and ourselves.

Throughout this book, you will learn how to:

1. **Identify Your Unique Superpowers:** Through various exercises and self-assessments, you will uncover which of the Clair-Senses are most dominant in you. Understanding these superpowers will allow you to harness their unique potential fully.
2. **Enhance Your Sensory Abilities**: With practical techniques and proven methods, you will strengthen

your Clair-Senses, enabling you to access deeper levels of intuition and insight that you never dreamed possible. You have this innately within you and it's time to know it and use it to make decisions that catapult your life in successful ways.

3. **Monetize Your Senses:** Learn how to apply your enhanced sensory abilities in ways that can benefit your professional life. Whether it's improving your communication skills, fostering better relationships, or finding new opportunities, your senses can be powerful tools for success by truly connecting with others and them seeing the value of you being in their lives.

4. **Apply Sensory Insights in Everyday Life:** From making better decisions to understanding the unspoken emotions of those around you, applying your sensory insights can transform your daily interactions and overall life experience.

As we journey through each chapter, you'll find a blend of scientific research, real-life stories, and practical exercises that make this book not only informative but also highly actionable. I am committed to helping you unlock and monetize your sensory superpowers, just as I have done in my own life.

Remember, these abilities are not exclusive to a select few. Everyone has the potential to develop and use their senses in extraordinary ways. By the end of this book, you will have the confidence and knowledge to own your genius and use your superpowers to create a life of abundance and fulfillment.

Let's embark on this expedition together, and may you discover the incredible power within you.

Thank you for embarking on this transformative journey with me. Your sensory superpowers await—let's unleash them!

With love and light – **Tammy De Mirza**
The Breakthrough Alchemist®

CHAPTER 1:
CLAIR-SENSES
A Journey to Self-Mastery

In the quiet moments when our known senses tell familiar tales, there exists a deeper narrative waiting to be discovered. Welcome to "Clair-Senses: A Journey to Self-Mastery," the first chapter of an exciting adventure. Here, the five senses merge with the mystical abilities called the Clairs—your hidden superpowers. This chapter invites you on an expedition to uncover the spiritual treasures that have been silently pulsating, waiting for the moment to be revealed.

You've used these senses your whole life, but now it's time to learn how you can use them, the benefits they offer, and techniques to develop them with purpose. This journey will boost your success in all areas of life.

As you begin this journey of sensory awakening, you'll understand yourself better by discovering how your senses truly work and learn to connect with others in amazing new ways. Imagine gaining insight into what people need to see, hear, smell, taste, or feel. It's like learning a superpower—

reading people and noticing the small clues they give before they even say a word. This journey will transform you, making you more aware and better at connecting and communicating with others.

As we navigate this voyage, diving deep into self-understanding, we discover that this isn't a straight path. Instead, it spirals deeper, connecting us with others in ways we never anticipated. The insights gained are not just about seeing things differently; they spark a transformation that changes how we interact with the world. This adventure will shape you in ways you never expected, opening new possibilities and connections.

At the edge of this transformation, we pause. We stand on the brink of a major change, like a butterfly about to emerge from its chrysalis. Let's get ready to embrace the exciting change ahead, full of endless possibilities. Imagine that thrilling and powerful moment when everything familiar fades away, and a new awareness takes over.

As we stand at this crossroads, it's important to recognize the incredible power and potential of this transformation. It's a call to not just understand but to experience life in a whole new way. This awakening can feel overwhelming because every sensation becomes stronger and every intuition sharper.

With these heightened senses, we are invited to step into the unknown and embrace the new aspects of ourselves. It's in this uncertain place where real growth happens. Here, we learn to use all our senses for deeper communication, stronger connections, and better understanding.

I know this journey well because I've walked this path. Imagine that life-changing moment—the kind that splits your life into 'before' and 'after.' It's a moment of deep realization, so powerful that the person you once were fades away. Suddenly, you're in a world where everything is intensified, where your senses are so sharp that the world around you feels both incredibly close and amazingly new. With this heightened awareness, there's a natural fear of the unknown as you stand on the edge of a self not yet fully understood but more connected to life than ever.

My name is Tammy, and I faced this crossroads at the age of eleven. That was when my reality shifted, drawing me into a world where my senses merged with something greater—the Clair-Senses.

One of my earliest memories of this big change at 11 involves a piece of music—a melody that used to move me but suddenly felt strange. I was sitting in the car, listening to a familiar song I loved, but I found myself feeling uneasy. Confused, I tried to understand why, and then it hit me: I had changed. The song was the same, but my connection to it wasn't. The 'old me' had enjoyed those notes, but the 'new me' didn't feel the same joy. It was a powerful sign that I had changed deeply and in a big way.

The shock and awe from this discovery stayed with me, leading me to study not only how our senses work but also to help thousands of people uncover theirs. I learned who they are, how they function, and how they naturally communicate and receive information, both physically and beyond. These senses reveal so much about us that we can't even imagine. Understanding them brings a newfound freedom and, most importantly, a deep love for oneself.

My simple joys were replaced with a new awareness that went beyond the ordinary. Friends, flavors, and melodies I once loved now felt different. I gained the ability to sense unspoken thoughts, see unseen energies, and hear unheard messages. These new gifts surfaced as if I had been reborn into a fresh, vibrant existence, as bright and clear as the dawn. You too can experience this as you learn who you are and how you function.

In this sacred dance, the sensory and the spiritual work together, each step a detailed movement toward self-discovery. The Clair-Senses Clairvoyance, Clairaudience, Clairgustance, Clairscent, and Clairsentience are the instruments of this dance, coming together to reveal the unseen forces that shape our lives and destinies.

Let's uncover the amazing powers our five senses reveal within the realm of the Clairs.

Clairvoyance: Beyond What the Eyes Can See

Clairvoyance is like having a super-powered version of sight. It lets you see beyond appearances to the true essence of things. It's the key to a deeper understanding, allowing you to look past the surface and into the heart of the matter. With Clairvoyance, you can pick up on the subtle details that others might miss. It helps you see the hidden truths and connect with what's there, going beyond what your eyes can see.

Clairaudience: Hearing the Melody Beyond Silence

Clairaudience is having super-sensitive hearing that goes beyond physical sounds. It tunes into the subtle vibrations and intentions that fill the silence. It's a deep superpower that helps Clairaudients listen in a way that also picks up on truths that words alone can't convey. This ability lets you hear the true essence of what's being said, understanding not just the words, but the intentions behind them, and not just the notes, but the symphony of the soul.

Clairgustance: Tasting the Invisible

Clairgustance goes beyond tasting flavors, allowing us to sense the true essence of our experiences and interactions with a deeper understanding and intuition. It invites us to savor life to its fullest, picking up on the subtle flavors of energies and emotions. This special sense lets us "taste" the very heart of our experiences, adding a richness that our tongues alone could never capture. By doing so, it provides us with a wealth of knowledge and insight, enriching our understanding of the world in a profound way.

Clairscent: The Scent of the Unseen

Clairscent is our ability to "smell" the unseen, picking up on the scents of change, opportunity, and sometimes, caution. It acts as an invisible guide, helping us navigate the aromatic hints of life's ever-changing paths. This sense helps us detect the fragrances of the nonphysical realm, sensing shifts, innovations, and warnings. It's like having a hidden compass that guides us through life's many crossroads.

Clairsentience: Feeling the Touch of Energy

Clairsentience is the empathic touch that feels the undercurrents of the world around us. It connects us to the energy and emotions that flow from every being, object, and space, providing a tactile sense of the universe's pulse. Clairsentience is the spiritual echo of our sense of touch, allowing us to feel the vibrations that ebb and flow around us. It amplifies our ability to empathize, connect, and truly feel the undercurrents of our interpersonal and energetic environments.

As we delve into the nuances of each of the five senses and their corresponding Clairs, you will learn to recognize the ones that resonate most with you. This awareness will enhance your communication skills, allowing you to express your truth with clarity and forge deep connections that touch the heart. Armed with this knowledge, you will stand apart, navigating social and professional landscapes with ease. The benefits will become quickly evident as you notice an increase in successful sales, improved workplace dynamics, promotions, and a newfound ability to engage with those who once seemed out of reach, all by mastering the art of meeting them on their communicative ground.

As we chart the course of this journey, you will learn not only to recognize these Clair-Senses but to embrace them as the powerful tools they are for navigating the complexities of the human experience. These senses become the foundation for building a life of clarity, connection, and purpose. They empower us to communicate with greater authenticity, to make decisions with confidence, and to engage with the world on a profoundly intimate level.

Through the cultivation of these senses, we begin to harmonize our inner and outer worlds, uniting the tangible with the ethereal. This harmony is the essence of self-mastery—a mastery that promises a richer, more abundant, and more aligned existence.

"Clair-Senses: A Journey to Self-Mastery" is an exploration, an education, and an evolution. With each step we take together, you'll peel away layers of the ordinary, revealing the extraordinary abilities that lie dormant within. This is your journey—a path that beckons you to become the architect of your destiny, a life replete with purpose, connection, and abundance.

To illustrate the complexity of navigating our senses without full awareness, let me recount a personal tale that underscores the essence of Clairsentience:

There was a time when I was 15, and life's clarity seemed a distant reality. My friend Terri called, overwhelmed by her storm of emotions. As I listened, offering guidance drawn from a place of intuition, I unknowingly began to shoulder her emotional burden. This invisible transfer was more than an act of empathy; it was a vivid lesson in the weight that our Clairsentient connections can carry. This encounter cast me into shadowed waters, a place far from my center.

It became a defining moment in my life, one where the murkiness of my feelings was a stark contrast to my usual state. It was not merely the distress of a friend that had unsettled me but the direct impact of my Clairsentience—the ability to feel deeply, which in that moment, became a conduit for her pain.

From this experience blossomed my deep understanding of Clairsentience and empathy. I discovered the art of navigating emotional undercurrents—not by absorbing them, but by recognizing them, acknowledging their origin, and gently deflecting them away from my emotional sphere. This skill, once honed, transformed how I interacted with the world; it became a beacon, guiding me through the fog of unspoken emotions and unseen energies, allowing me to observe, understand, and ultimately, maintain my equilibrium while offering support.

You stand at the threshold of a significant transformation. This book is a compilation of comprehensive studies on the top five Clair-Senses, fashioned to enlighten, engage, and empower your journey. What follows is a glimpse into what you will discover in each chapter, with each specific Clair represented. However, this is not limited to just these points—we will uncover much more along the way.

Definition and Discovery: This segment serves as your gateway to the world of Clair-Senses, exploring each sense and its distinct manifestations within you. It provides a comprehensive introduction to these extraordinary abilities, detailing how they can vary from person to person and influence your perception and interaction with the world. As you embark on this journey, you will uncover the foundational elements that define Clair-Senses, enhancing your ability to tap into deeper spiritual dimensions and enrich your sensory experiences.

Locating the Senses: Discover the physical and energetic epicenters within your body where Clair-Senses thrive. This segment guides you through the process of identifying these crucial points, enhancing your understanding of how and where these senses operate. By learning to recognize and activate these centers, you will be equipped to more effectively harness and cultivate your Clair-Senses, leading to improved spiritual awareness and personal empowerment.

Benefits of Awareness: Dive into the profound impacts of developing an awareness of your Clair-Senses. This segment highlights the transformative effects that such awareness can have on your life, from deepening personal relationships to expanding your understanding of the universe. By fostering this heightened sense of awareness, you will unlock the potential for a richer, more connected life, filled with meaningful insights and spiritual fulfillment.

The Challenges Unseen: Address the common obstacles and challenges that may arise as you explore and develop your Clair-Senses. This segment discusses the potential misunderstandings and missteps that can occur without proper guidance and knowledge, offering strategies for overcoming these hurdles. By preemptively identifying and addressing these issues, you will be better prepared to navigate the complexities of your spiritual journey with clarity and confidence.

History of Clair-senses: Delve into the rich historical context of Clair senses in this segment, tracing their recognition and utilization across different cultures and epochs. From ancient shamanic practices to the mystical traditions of the Middle Ages, and up to modern parapsychology, you will explore how various societies have understood and employed these extrasensory perceptions. The segment will highlight key historical figures, seminal texts, and pivotal moments that have shaped the understanding of Clair-Senses. By appreciating the historical depth of these abilities, you gain a broader perspective on their significance and the evolutionary role they have played in human development. This historical overview not only adds depth to your knowledge but also illustrates the timeless relevance and potential of Clair-Senses in human evolution.

Historical Figures with Clair Senses: Explore the lives and legacies of historical figures renowned for their sensory superpowers. This segment delves into the profound influence these abilities had on their contributions to society and culture. By examining how these figures harnessed their Clair-Senses, you will gain insight into the powerful impact such abilities can have on personal achievements and societal advancements, inspiring you to explore and develop your sensory capabilities.

Origins and Indications of Clair-Senses: This segment explores the initial signs and developmental origins of the Clairs, providing insights into how these abilities manifest and evolve. Understanding the early indicators can help you identify and nurture your sensory superpowers effectively. You'll learn about the common experiences and phenomena that suggest the awakening or presence of these senses, allowing for a deeper comprehension of their roles in your personal and spiritual growth. This knowledge equips you with the ability to foster these abilities from their nascent stages into full maturity, enhancing your overall sensory perception and spiritual connectivity.

Detecting Clair-Senses in Others: This segment will teach you how to recognize and understand the presence of Clair-Senses in others. By learning to detect these sensory abilities, you can better comprehend the subtle energies and signals that people emit. This awareness can enhance interpersonal interactions, allowing for more empathetic and intuitive communication. You'll learn techniques for sensing the specific Clair-Senses at work in others, which can be especially valuable in personal relationships, therapeutic settings, and team dynamics in the workplace. Practical exercises and indicators will be provided to help you cultivate this perceptive skill, enriching your connections with a deeper level of understanding and mutual respect.

Development and Mastery: This segment focuses on the advanced techniques and practices for refining your Clair-Senses to achieve mastery. This segment provides a roadmap for transforming your budding abilities into a profound skillset. Through practical exercises and expert advice, you will learn how to elevate your Clair-Senses from mere potential to a vital component of your daily life and spiritual practice, leading to greater self-awareness and life mastery.

Communication with Clair-Senses: Uncover the revolutionary impact that Clair-Senses can have on communication. This segment examines how these enhanced senses can transform interactions, making them more empathetic, intuitive, and effective. By integrating Clair-Senses into your communication practices, you not only improve how you connect with others but also foster deeper relationships, ensuring that your exchanges go beyond the surface to touch the essence of those involved.

Monetizing Clair-Senses in Personal Relationships and Careers: This segment focuses on how you can leverage your Clair-Senses to enrich and advance your personal relationships and professional life. By honing your sensory abilities, you can create deeper connections, foster trust, and enhance communication in personal interactions. In the realm of careers, these enhanced sensory perceptions can lead to better decision-making, increased creativity, and unique leadership qualities. Practical tips and strategies will be discussed to show how understanding and applying your Clair-Senses can be a valuable asset in not only improving personal fulfillment but also in achieving professional success and financial prosperity.

Each chapter in this book is designed to not only educate but also inspire you to explore and enhance your sensory capabilities, providing practical insights and historical anecdotes that underscore the profound impact of Clair-Senses throughout history.

Thank you for embarking on this transformative journey with me. I hope that these pages will be a beacon, guiding you inward to embrace the art of self-love—not merely as a concept, but as the pinnacle of mastery. Together, we shall weave through the rich tapestry of your Clair-Senses, unlocking the robust strength and boundless potential that awaits within, steering you towards a life brimming with fulfillment and awe.

Are you prepared to embark on this exquisite voyage? To harness the profound and unseen, to step boldly into the vastness of your true being? The path illuminated by the Clair-Senses stretches out before us, a hallowed trail woven with the enchantment of your spirit's essence. With hearts wide open to the whispers of our intuition and minds receptive to the lessons of the soul, we begin the sacred dance of self-mastery.

As we stand poised on the brink of discovery, let us move forward with eager anticipation and minds thirsting for knowledge. The exploration of Clairvoyance is merely the first step—the gateway to the grand adventure that lies ahead. I will be with you, guiding you, as we journey through each revelation and insight. Together, let's set forth on this path to mastery.

Your sensory superpowers await—let's unleash them!

CHAPTER 2:
CLAIRVOYANCE
Beyond Sight

Welcome to a journey into the profound depths of Clairvoyance, an intriguing ability that transcends ordinary perception and unveils the unseen layers of reality. This chapter will explore how Clairvoyance is not merely about predicting the future or communicating with the nonphysical; it's about enhancing your understanding of the world around you.

By delving into the signs of this extraordinary ability and its significant implications for personal and professional relationships, we'll discover how Clairvoyance can serve as a powerful tool in navigating life's complexities, enhancing decision-making, and fostering deeper connections. Join us as we unlock the secrets of this innate superpower and learn how to harness its potential to transform your perception and enrich your life.

When you hear the term Clairvoyance, you might think of crystal balls and fortune-tellers, but it is far deeper than that. It is an innate superpower that offers the ability to see beyond the five senses, to perceive information and insights from the nonphysical realm. This chapter explores the signs of this ability, its implications for personal and professional relationships, and how it can be an asset in your life.

Clairvoyance is an extraordinary ability to see the physical world in a much more profound way. It's also a window into the nonphysical world, giving you access to information and insights that regular senses can't. It's a fantastic superpower that opens both physical and nonphysical realities to you and is so useful to help you make decisions that are beneficial not only to you but to everyone.

To address the physical aspect of this sense, you will find that you can access and gain information intuitively by noticing what is going on in your physical reality. This is not only noticing the person in front of you but being able to also see things that are happening around you with others at the same time. It's almost like you've been given a special agent's training with the CIA. You notice things that others don't.

This ability sharpens your awareness to notice subtle cues such as eye movements, facial expressions, and overall body language, enabling you to catch details that others miss. You become skilled at spotting when someone's attention shifts—whether they're losing interest or showing signs of boredom or displeasure, such as eye-rolling. This heightened sensitivity lets you accurately gauge how engaged your audience is. By tuning into these signals, you gain valuable insights that guide your interactions, helping you choose the best approach based on the unique cues you pick up. You start to understand not just what people say and do, but also their unspoken language—revealing what they truly feel and think beyond what you can see and hear.

People constantly give you signals that show how a conversation is affecting them. For example, crossed arms might mean that someone is closing off, feeling defensive, or simply resting. Noticing these details helps you to interpret what their actions say about the conversation and how well you're communicating. Developing the keen ability to focus on these cues is crucial to becoming more perceptive and therefore, reaching people on a much deeper level by engaging in ways that create that environment. By paying attention to and responding to these signs, you can improve your interactions and overall life experience. This practice of careful observation not only helps you understand others better but also empowers you to respond more thoughtfully and effectively.

As an added benefit to my clients, I help them create transformational changes, by teaching them to develop their senses further. Life is a game that we play, and the physical world gives you the visible signs, and the ability to hear, taste, smell, and feel the symptoms that you unconsciously create with your thoughts. The world constantly shows you the signs of what you are thinking, whether you are aware of them or not. The problems (which I call predicaments), or symptoms you are experiencing are there to reveal what your thoughts and the energy behind them are creating. Learning how to detect these signs, and how to see them, is crucial for deciding if you want to keep what is happening in your life. This intel is the pathway to changing your life by changing your mind. This is a powerful way to use this ability.

You can use your sight to sense how your world feels to you and to gather information to make clear and sound decisions that are in alignment with what you truly desire. When something doesn't feel good, it is out of alignment for you, isn't your truth, and will never feel good. When you use the physical to see what is before you, then you use your sense of Clairsentience to feel it, you'll know, is this aligned with who I am and what I want? If it is, then great, create more of it, but if it isn't, then use the discomfort to make new choices and get what you want. (Note that I cannot go in-depth, because of the scope of this book to teach you conscious alchemy, but if you are interested in creating what you want at will, refer to the Free Resources page to get a free Masterclass on Manifesting and you can book a discovery call with me on my website).

The Laws of Attraction are clear about this and this is what I teach clients: You experience that which you do not want, to know what you want. Therefore, it is wise to pay attention to what is happening and decide whether it resonates or not. If it doesn't, you can change your mind, to create a new trajectory in your life.

Everything is energy and can be changed. Everything that you use in your daily life was created by someone's attention and energy being put into it enough, that it became matter. You have the power to do the same, create things you want by focusing on them.

To help you along this journey, take a moment and answer the following questions:

1. What is the physical showing you?
2. Do you like what you are seeing?
3. What would you change, what do you want to see?

4. What decisions will you make based on the physical signs of what you think?
5. Will you take the steps forward with this new decision and be a part of the change?

As you develop your ability to interpret physical and emotional signals through Clairsentience, it's important to recognize the role of Clairvoyance in this process. This superpower extends this sensory understanding to a higher level, offering a more comprehensive view of both seen and unseen energies. This transition from sensing immediate physical realities to perceiving subtle energies and intentions highlights how both abilities complement each other. Together, they empower you to navigate life's complexities with greater awareness and precision."

To sum it up, Clairvoyance is a bridge between the visible and invisible. It goes beyond the ordinary, allowing you to see not only the unseen dimensions of the nonphysical world but also the subtle aspects of your physical reality that others might miss. This ability gives you a wealth of insight, providing important information that helps guide your decisions and reveal paths that aren't obvious to the naked eye. It's not just a mystical talent; it's a practical tool for navigating life with wisdom and intuition. Those who develop this ability gain access to a wider range of knowledge, often seeing things clearly that others can't. This leads to a deeper understanding of what to do in the present moment, thanks to the ability to see both the world and the choices that shape it.

In the nonphysical sense, you might see things that others can't—like glimpses, energies, outlines, or even through remote viewing. Keep reading to find out the signs that you have this ability.

Here is an Overview of the History of Clairvoyance

Clairvoyance has a long and intertwined history with various cultural and spiritual traditions around the world, dating back to ancient times.

In ancient civilizations, Clairvoyance, or the ability to perceive events and information beyond the normal range of the senses, has been recorded in many ancient cultures. The term itself comes from the French words Clair (clear) and voyance (vision), but the concept predates this terminology by millennia.

The Egyptians and Mesopotamians had oracles and seers who were believed to receive visions from the gods, providing guidance and prophecies. These were often ritualized and played significant roles in decisions made by leaders.

In the Greeks and Romans, the Oracle of Delphi is one of the most famous examples of Clairvoyance in the ancient world. The Pythia, a priestess at the Temple of Apollo at Delphi, served as a medium through whom the gods communicated. People from all over the Greek world, including kings, would consult her on everything from important state matters to personal affairs.

During the Middle Ages and the Renaissance, Clairvoyance was often associated with witchcraft and heresy, especially in Europe. The fear of the supernatural led to many Clairvoyants being persecuted under the suspicion of witchcraft.

John Dee, an advisor to Queen Elizabeth I, used crystal gazing to receive visions that he believed were angelic messages helping to guide the monarchy.

The 19th century saw a revival of interest in Clairvoyance within the context of the spiritualist movement in both America and Europe.

Spiritualism marked a significant turning point where Clairvoyance was more openly discussed and practiced. It became a common practice in séances, where mediums claimed to see and communicate with the spirits of the dead.

With Theosophy, founders like Helena Blavatsky spoke of Clairvoyance as part of the broader abilities humans could develop. Theosophy helped popularize Eastern spiritual concepts, including those involving psychic abilities, in the Western world.

With Parapsychology in the 20th century, the study of Clairvoyance entered a more scientific realm with the establishment of parapsychology. Researchers like J.B. Rhine at Duke University conducted experiments to test the veracity of Clairvoyance and other psychic phenomena under controlled conditions.

Today, Clairvoyance is often associated with New Age and spiritual practices. It is widely discussed in the context of personal spiritual growth and psychic development.

Clairvoyance and other psychic abilities are also popular themes in entertainment and literature.

Throughout its history, Clairvoyance has been both revered and feared, viewed as a gift from the gods or a dangerous power. Its perception is largely influenced by cultural and spiritual beliefs about the nature of reality and human capabilities.

Famous Historical Figure with Clairvoyance

Michel de Nostredame, better known as Nostradamus, is one of the most famous figures associated with Clairvoyance. Born in 1503 in Saint-Rémy-de-Provence, France, Nostradamus is best known for his book "Les Prophéties," first published in 1555. This collection of poetic quatrains is believed to predict future events and has been widely interpreted and debated over the centuries.

Nostradamus used a mix of astrological calculations and his own visionary experiences to foresee the future. He claimed to induce these visions through meditation, often working at night in a secluded room. Using a bowl of water or a "magic mirror," he practiced scrying, a method allowing him to "see" into the future or access hidden information—traits commonly linked with Clairvoyance.

Despite the cryptic and often vague language of his quatrains, Nostradamus's legacy as a Clairvoyant has endured. His prophecies are credited with predicting major world events, from the Great Fire of London to the rise of Adolf Hitler, and even events as recent as the 9/11 attacks. His legacy highlights humanity's deep fascination with Clairvoyance and the desire to understand and predict the future.

Nostradamus also exemplifies the skepticism often associated with Clairvoyants. While many believe in his predictive powers, others argue that his writings are too broad or interpreted to fit historical events after they happen. Regardless, his impact on cultural and esoteric circles as a Clairvoyant remains significant.

Nostradamus and his practices show us the historical roots of Clairvoyance, not just as entertainment or curiosity, but as a profound ability believed to provide insight into the nature of our reality.

An interesting side story is that when I lived in Agen, France, studying with the most famous Trompe l'oeil artist of our generation, I saw a sign while driving home that read: "Home of Nostradamus". I was thrilled and intrigued, and since it was close to the end of my stay, I decided to visit the place where he had lived. This was to be my last weekend in France, and I couldn't think of a better way to spend it.

I walked the distance, which I later found out was more than three miles. Thankfully, the place was open. I saw Nostradamus's picture on the wall and felt a deep connection, seeing beyond the physical and gaining insight into who he was when he lived there. I used my sensory superpowers as I'm teaching you to do. His life was simple during that period, and he used the land to provide for his family. The information that I received was telling and beautiful to me personally and I teared up at receiving things beyond the normal. I knew he had lived in the bottom of the property, that he wasn't good at farming, but was trying his hand at it. I knew intuitively that the animals slept above them to keep them warm. l also was getting the discernment that this place had represented another life to him, it was calm, but I also sensed intense pain. I wanted to stand for an hour and just stare into his eyes but was approached by someone in the restaurant and ushered to a table.

Superpowers Unleashed!

I had the amazing opportunity to sit and chat with the owner, who thankfully spoke fluent English. We talked about the property she had bought and was now operating a restaurant in. The conversation with the owner was beautiful and engaging. Over a cappuccino, she explained that Nostradamus had married a woman from Agen and had two sons, all of whom died from the plague. She took me on a personal tour of where they had lived and I saw with my physical eyes, what I had seen by looking at his picture, the bottom floor where he had lived. It was as if time and space were frozen, I could hear the animals who lived above them to keep the family warm and had that confirmed by the owner. I was able to read the energy of their lives together. Due to the immense loss in his life, Nostradamus left shortly after their deaths. It was a small place but adequately served him during that time in his life. I could feel that his life took an entirely different direction after that.

I promised to return during the week with another American who had come to study with the famous artist Michel Nadai. We visited for dinner on Tuesday, just before I left France on Friday. It was a fabulous parting meal and surreal being there, feeling and sensing the energy of the space.

When you use your sensory superpowers, magnificent experiences happen for you like this one for me. This is a great reason to develop them so that you will receive more than you imagined. For we are not just confined to what is in this physical world and being able to tap into these abilities, expands our knowledge, feelings, and perception of life. It's just one of the benefits of using them to gather information.

Where is it located?

Clairvoyance is a term that suggests incredible insight but goes beyond the traditional five senses. It blends the ability to see both the physical and metaphysical worlds. This unique skill uses our physical eyes to observe the external world and combines it with the intuitive vision of the third eye, located between your eyebrows. The third eye is believed to see through the veils of physical reality, offering glimpses into realms beyond the ordinary. This merging of the seen and unseen is where Clairvoyance truly shines. It provides not just physical observation but a deeper understanding and insight into the information that unfolds before us, both visible and sensed. With Clairvoyance, you can perceive hidden truths and gain profound insights that enhance your awareness and guide your decisions in life.

Common Beginnings of Clairvoyance

1. **Spontaneous Visions:** You might experience spontaneous visions that come unexpectedly. These can occur in both the waking state and in dreams. You might see clear images or scenes play out when you close your eyes or even while interacting with your everyday environment.

2. **Sight:** You might experience something in the periphery of your eyes, like the corners of your eyes, you see movement, but when you look directly, it isn't there. You may often question if you are going crazy or if you saw something. YOU DID!

3. **Childhood Experiences:** Many Clairvoyants notice abilities from a young age, often dismissing them as imagination or daydreams. Children might report seeing people or animals that others cannot see or knowing information that they have not been told. Such as having an imaginary friend.

4. **Heightened Sensitivity:** A heightened sense of awareness is common. This might be sensitivity to physical environments, emotions, or even the energy of

a room. Clairvoyants often report a feeling of being able to 'read' the places or people around them more deeply than others.

5. **Trigger Events:** For some, Clairvoyance begins after a significant life event such as a near-death experience, serious illness, or a profound emotional trauma. These events can trigger a shift in perception that opens Clairvoyant abilities.

6. **Meditative and Spiritual Practices:** Engaging in practices that promote connection to your inner self and the universe—like meditation, yoga, or various spiritual disciplines—can also awaken Clairvoyant abilities. These practices often help in quieting the mind, which may make it easier to perceive subtle energies and visions.

7. **Lucid Dreaming:** You may begin experiencing Clairvoyant abilities during lucid dreams, where you consciously manipulate and control your dream environments. These vivid dreams can be a playground for Clairvoyant visions, allowing you to see and interact with symbols, people, or events that provide insight into your waking life.

8. **Synchronicities:** Frequent encounters with synchronicities—meaningful coincidences that seem

too timely to be a mere chance—can signal the awakening of Clairvoyant abilities. These synchronicities may appear as repeated numbers, names, or visual motifs that seem to offer guidance or messages from the universe.

9. **Aura Sight:** Developing the ability to see auras, or the energy fields that surround people, animals, and even objects, can be a sign of burgeoning Clairvoyant abilities. This may start with you seeing simple glows or colors around others and can evolve into more detailed perceptual experiences.

10. **Psychic Flashes:** You might experience sudden, flash-like visions that come without warning. These flashes can provide brief glimpses into future events or reveal hidden truths about a situation or person.

11. **Connection with Nature:** An increased intuitive connection with natural elements—such as plants, animals, or weather patterns—can also mark the beginning of Clairvoyant experiences. You may feel as if you can communicate with or receive messages from nature, offering you insights and wisdom.

Recognizing these common beginnings of Clairvoyance is crucial for anyone exploring their sensory potential. Whether through spontaneous visions, heightened sensitivities, or profound meditative practices, each sign can serve as a stepping stone to deeper spiritual understanding and insight. As you become aware of these initial manifestations, it is important to nurture them with an open heart and a curious mind. Embrace these experiences as part of your unique spiritual journey, encouraging growth and development in your Clairvoyant abilities. With patience and practice, these beginnings can unfold into a rich tapestry of psychic and sensory awareness that enhances every aspect of your life, opening doors to new dimensions of perception and connection.

Signs of Emerging Clairvoyance

1. **Visual Flashes:** Seeing flashes of light or brief images that are not physically present. These might include colors, symbols, or scenes that flash momentarily before the eyes.
2. **Seeing Auras:** The ability to see a field of energy (auras) surrounding people, animals, or even plants. This might start as seeing simple white outlines and evolve into seeing more detailed hues.
3. **Precognition:** Experiencing premonitions about future events that come to pass. These can be vivid and

detailed or simply a sense of knowing what is about to happen.

4. **Seeing Spirits or Entities:** Encounters with spiritual entities or deceased persons not visible to others.

5. **Intuitive Insights:** Suddenly knowing information about people or situations without knowing how or why you know it. This might involve details about someone's life, thoughts, or feelings that you couldn't have known through normal means.

Understanding and acknowledging these signs and experiences can be the first step towards embracing and honing your Clairvoyant abilities.

Signs you have Clairvoyance

Symptoms or signs of Clairvoyance can vary among individuals, but typically include the following experiences which indicate a heightened intuitive ability to receive visual or sensory information beyond what is perceived by the ordinary senses:

1. **Visions:** Receiving clear, visual mental images of objects, symbols, events, or scenes that are not physically present.

2. **Precognition:** Having foreknowledge of events through visions or dreams before they happen.
3. **Remote Viewing:** Being able to describe or give details about a place or event that is out of the line of sight because you are there, watching it as if it is currently happening, even though you are here in the present.
4. **Seeing Auras:** Perceiving colors or light around people, animals, or objects that others cannot see.
5. **Spiritual Encounters:** Seeing or sensing spirits, guides, or angelic beings that are not visible to others.
6. **Symbolic Dreams:** Experiencing dreams with vivid imagery that may carry messages or foretell future events.
7. **Peripheral Visions:** Detecting movement or seeing shapes and shadows out of the corner of the eye.
8. **Third Eye Activity:** Feeling pressure, tingling, or a sensation of opening in the area of the forehead between the eyebrows.
9. **Sudden Insights:** Receiving spontaneous insights or solutions to problems without a logical basis for

them. You might wake up with a ng what to do and how to fix something you couldn't figure out before.

10. **Seeing Patterns or Synchronicities:** Recognizing patterns or synchronicities in life that seem to guide or signal important messages. Such as noticing if there are events that repeat themselves.

11. **Déjà Vu:** Experiencing strong sensations of having already seen or experienced a current situation, and even sometimes knowing how the conversation will end and who will say what next.

12. **Daydreams:** Having intense daydreams that feel as real as life and may provide information about future events.

13. **Psychic Flashes:** Experiencing sudden flashes of insight or understanding about situations or people.

14. **Insightful:** By watching the world around you, you gather information that is invaluable to you, making you feel clear about what is going on, taking away insecurities, questioning yourself, and making decisions with discernment.

15. **Vivid Dreams:** Dreams that are not only clear and memorable but seem real, and carry significance or foresight. There is a significant difference between having these dreams and having others.

16. **Third Eye Sensations:** A feeling of pressure, tingling, or pulsing between the eyebrows, often associated with the 'third eye' where Clairvoyance is said to reside.
17. **Natural Affinity:** A strong, natural affinity for psychic practices, spiritual studies, or metaphysical concepts, even if you haven't actively pursued or studied them.
18. **Spontaneous Knowledge:** Suddenly knowing things about strangers — like their intentions or life details — without any logical way of knowing.
19. **Precise Premonitions:** Experiencing premonitions about events or feelings about situations that turn out to be accurate.
20. **Symbolic Language:** An intuitive understanding of the symbolic language that appears in your mind or your dreams, and an innate ability to interpret it.
21. **Spontaneous Information:** Feeling as though you are receiving messages or guidance, even when no one is around, especially when these messages pertain to future events or provide insight into current situations.

22. **Sudden Sensations:** Sensitivity to energy shifts in a room or around people, even if there is no apparent change to others.
23. **Synchronicities:** Experiencing frequent synchronicities or 'meaningful coincidences' that seem to guide or warn you.
24. **Affirmations from Reality:** Receiving affirmations from reality, such as seeing relevant numbers, words, or events that seem to answer your thoughts or questions.

These symptoms of Clairvoyance might not only be experienced visually but also as a sense of knowing. It's important to note that Clairvoyance and its signs are deeply personal and can vary in intensity and frequency. Individuals who experience these symptoms often describe them as sporadic and not within their control, at least initially. Many people with Clairvoyant abilities choose to develop them further through practices such as meditation, psychic or spiritual development exercises, and learning from experts who teach them personally what to do and how to own these abilities.

Examples of Clairvoyance with real stories

I was once in a session with my daughter and we spoke for a little while before we officially began the session. After a few minutes of catching up. I asked her if she was ready to begin the session, to which she answered yes. I started to hear that she was outside and asked her what she was doing, and she said that she had decided to take a walk. I was concerned about her being in a private space and expressed that. However, I began to see the entire conversation playing out in a way I'd never seen before.

As I was speaking to her, I was vividly describing where she was when we began the conversation on Washington Street, close to the Cleveland Park area and zoo, and coming up to the traffic light. I described the scene from the moment we got on the phone and, that while speaking, she had turned left at the light and bore to the right, then took the next left, turned right into the picnic parking area, and parked the third parking space to the right. She then walked across the field where we used to go on picnics when she was little and played frisbee and threw softballs. She had then taken a left and was about to step onto the bridge to cross the river. As she stepped onto the bridge, I said "Speak to the couple who is about to join you on the bridge".

She was in shock and asked me what I was doing, she'd never experienced this before, and little did she know, I never had either. We both were in shock. I again said, "Look, the couple is about to step left onto the bridge, put the phone down by your side and speak to them". She did so and as soon as they walked past her, I saw her turn right and knew exactly where she was going and knew she'd be in a quiet space to hear the session. My Clairvoyant sight stopped and this technique is called remote viewing.

Another example is a client of mine who was in a session on a Tuesday morning, and I asked her who was coming into the office on Friday, and that she needed to get an audience with him. I explained that he was three levels above her current manager, but she needed to be with him, and that this meeting would help her career. She didn't want to do this, because of the ramifications of going above her manager's head to see this man. However, when I told her specifically the name of the lady to approach and what to say to her to get time on his schedule, she agreed to do it, laughing about me knowing the assistant's name. It was the evidence she needed to see her way to doing what was being given to her.

She called me back within minutes and was excited that it worked, she had an appointment with him but still didn't see why this was being given at this moment, and I asked her to trust the process. I then began to teach her how to use her Clairvoyance abilities to see and to know the signs of what was about to transpire with him. I asked her to look for the signs that he was engaging with her and that if it was going well, he would give her 30-35 minutes if she was reaching him. While in the meeting, she watched carefully, paying attention to her Clairvoyant abilities and they spent 32 minutes together, it was fun, and easy, and created a new connection because of the intuitive information she received and honored.

On Friday after their meeting, my client called me excitedly telling me that the meeting went well, that she had a great time and enjoyed herself immensely, and felt good about everything that had happened. Because of her honoring her abilities and paying attention to her inner guidance of knowing what to say, she was promoted three times within three months because he saw her.

You can see from using these examples, that if you look beyond what is seen, you will also be tuned into what is happening before you on a deeper level. You can see the seen and the unseen with Clairvoyance and all the information is telling and useful.

Benefits of Seeing in Communication

In Relationships:

As you just saw from the example, Clairvoyance can greatly improve how we connect with others by allowing a deeper understanding beyond normal conversations. Being able to perceive non-verbal cues, energies, and unspoken thoughts offers a unique edge in all relationships.

A Clairvoyant has an innate knowledge of emotional intelligence and can sense the emotions and feelings of others, which allows for compassionate and personalized responses. This heightened emotional intelligence can strengthen bonds and create more meaningful connections.

By foreseeing potential misunderstandings and identifying the root causes of conflicts, a Clairvoyant can address issues before they escalate, promoting harmony in relationships. Seeing things from another's perspective can foster empathy and understanding, leading to more supportive and nurturing relationships.

In Monetizing:

In the business realm, Clairvoyance can be a valuable asset by helping you make strategic decisions based on insights into market trends, consumer behavior, and competitive dynamics that others might miss.

Clairvoyants can offer their services to individuals or businesses guiding on various matters, from personal life decisions to business strategies. You become a valuable consultant to others because of the insights you see and perceive.

With the superpower to perceive the unspoken, you can navigate negotiations with a level of foresight, ensuring better outcomes and potential gains in financial dealings. This unique advantage can be monetized, turning Clairvoyance into a profitable skill in the business world.

Getting Clarity on Others:

Discerning the true intentions and integrity of others can protect you from deception, ensuring trust in both personal and professional relationships.

By understanding the specific needs and preferences of another person, you can tailor your communication to be more effective and appreciated.

This ability allows you to connect with people on a deeper level and that makes people want to be around you and do business with you.

Cultivating Clairvoyance for Growth:

Regularly practicing mindfulness and meditative techniques can enhance Clairvoyance, making your perceptions clearer and more accurate.

Sharing your insights with others and getting feedback can help you interpret your Clairvoyant experiences more accurately.

Engaging with books and courses on Clairvoyance and psychic development can provide you with tools and techniques to harness this ability more effectively.

Expanding Clairvoyant Abilities:

Regularly practice visualization exercises to enhance your mental imagery and ability to see beyond the physical.

Learning and practicing energy work, such as Reiki and other modalities, can increase sensitivity to the energies around you and improve your Clairvoyant abilities.

Joining groups or communities that focus on psychic and spiritual development can provide support and shared experiences, speeding up your personal growth.

By incorporating these practices, Clairvoyance can not only improve personal relationships but also open avenues for professional growth and financial opportunities.

Potential Challenges of Clairvoyance if Mismanaged or Unrecognized

Having Clairvoyance can bring a unique set of challenges and issues that might affect people who possess or develop these abilities. Here are some potential issues that Clairvoyants may face:

1. Receiving constant or intense Clairvoyant information can be overwhelming, leading to sensory overload or mental exhaustion.
2. Clairvoyants might sometimes find it challenging to differentiate between their visions and physical reality, which can be disorienting or lead to confusion.
3. Seeing and feeling energies or spirits, especially those associated with negative experiences or

emotions, can have a profound emotional impact and may lead to anxiety or fear.

4. Clairvoyants may unintentionally access private information about others, leading to ethical dilemmas and concerns about privacy.

5. There is always a risk of misinterpreting Clairvoyant insights, which can result in making incorrect decisions or passing on misinformation.

6. Encountering skepticism or outright disbelief from others can lead to feelings of isolation or self-doubt for Clairvoyants.

7. There may be social stigma attached to your seeing abilities, which can affect personal and professional relationships and lead to social isolation.

8. Clairvoyants may question their mental health, especially when they begin to experience supernatural phenomena, due to the fear of being labeled as delusional or mentally unstable.

9. Some individuals report physical symptoms associated with Clairvoyant experiences, such as headaches or fatigue, particularly around the third-eye area.

10. Friends and family might have trouble understanding or accepting the Clairvoyant's

experiences, which can strain or complicate relationships.

11. Clairvoyants may find it difficult to establish and keep boundaries between their feelings and those they sense from others, leading to emotional entanglement or a sense of intrusion.
12. There is a significant responsibility in handling the information gained through Clairvoyance, including ethical considerations about when and how you share it.
13. A strong focus on Clairvoyant visions can sometimes distract from living in the present moment and attending to the immediate, practical aspects of life.
14. Others may have unrealistic expectations of your Clairvoyant abilities, assuming they are infallible or that you can solve all problems, which can lead to pressure and stress.
15. Some may struggle to accept your Clairvoyant abilities, particularly if they conflict with their cultural or personal beliefs, but it is one of your greatest assets, and using it personally is the most profound gift you can give to yourself and others. Consider that the information you receive is not

available for all, and that makes you unique and they don't have to understand.

16. Often, Clairvoyants will use their ability to detect things for others, but not for themselves. The abilities that you have are on purpose, you earned them, and using them for yourself is the highest use of them because what is good for you, is good for others when it comes to making decisions because of your intuition.

Clairvoyants often benefit from learning how to manage their abilities and find the balance to avoid these potential issues. This can involve setting healthy boundaries that nurture your needs, developing coping strategies, and seeking support from understanding communities. The most important step to consider is obtaining guidance from a highly developed Clairvoyant who can teach you the ins and outs of who they are personally and be able to assimilate the information in an easy, cohesive way to create success.

A skilled Clairvoyant mentor can guide you home to who you authentically are, understand how you want to use these supernatural abilities effectively, and support you as you learn to navigate life with these special abilities. These offerings and much more, including techniques that are individually designed just for you to use to develop these further and understand why things happen, would be based on many factors that only the seasoned Clairvoyant can detect. I am here for you if you want to know more! Refer to the Free Resources page at the back of the book.

Career Paths for Clairvoyants

Professional Psychic or Medium: Clairvoyants can work as professional psychics or mediums, providing personal readings to help individuals gain insights into their past, present, and future. This can include career advice, relationship guidance, spiritual and self-development.

Life Coaching and Counseling: Using their Clairvoyant abilities, they can excel in life coaching or counseling roles, where they can help clients navigate personal challenges and transitions by providing deeper insights that the clients themselves may not be aware of.

Holistic Health Practitioner: Clairvoyants can integrate their skills into practices like reiki, acupuncture, or other holistic health modalities. Their ability to see energies and auras can enhance their effectiveness in diagnosing and treating their clients' physical or emotional imbalances.

Creative Arts: Many Clairvoyants find that their ability to visualize and foresee outcomes enhances their creativity. They may pursue careers as artists, writers, or designers, using their visions to inspire and inform their work.

Corporate Strategist or Consultant: Clairvoyants can offer valuable insights into business trends and human dynamics, making them excellent strategic planners or business consultants. Their ability to foresee potential outcomes can be crucial for risk management and strategic planning in corporate environments.

Paranormal Researcher: Those with Clairvoyant abilities may be drawn to roles that involve investigating the paranormal or unexplained phenomena. This can include working with organizations that study psychic phenomena or contributing to academic research in parapsychology.

Workshop and Retreat Leader: Clairvoyants can organize workshops or retreats to teach others how to develop their psychic abilities or to share their insights on spiritual and metaphysical topics. These events can also serve as healing retreats, where Clairvoyants guide participants through personal growth experiences.

Motivational Speaker: Given their unique insights and experiences, Clairvoyants can become effective motivational speakers, sharing their knowledge and inspiring others to explore and develop their intuitive abilities.

Law Enforcement Consultant: Some Clairvoyants work with law enforcement agencies to help solve crimes by providing psychic insights that may not be otherwise obtainable through traditional methods.

Historical Researcher: Clairvoyants with a strong ability to see into the past can contribute to historical research, providing details that may not be documented in physical records. Their visions can offer a different perspective on historical events.

These career paths showcase how Clairvoyants can utilize their unique abilities in various fields, offering them opportunities to both develop their skills and contribute meaningfully to society.

Detecting Clairvoyance in Others

Recognizing Clairvoyant abilities in others allows for deeper interaction and understanding. Here's how you might detect Clairvoyance:

Observational Signs:

A person might make remarks or have insights that seem beyond natural intuition or guesswork.

They may appear to be focusing on something that isn't physically present or looking beyond the obvious.

Notice if they often seem to catch something in their peripheral vision or react to something unseen.

Behavioral Indicators:

They may speak of events before they happen or know things with no logical explanation.

A strong reaction to someone else's emotional state, even when that person hasn't verbally expressed their feelings, can be a sign.

Might discuss dreams that have an uncanny resemblance to actual events or contain deep insights.

Communicating with a Clairvoyant Individual:

Be clear and honest in your communications. Clairvoyants may pick up on what you're not saying as much as what you are.

Engage in discussions about metaphysical topics which can create a supportive environment for them to share their experiences.

Validate their experiences without judgment, which can encourage open and honest communication about their insights.

Helping Others Understand Clairvoyant Messages:

Use language that is relatable and grounded. Instead of saying, "I see a spirit," one might say, "I sense a strong presence or energy that could represent..."

Share practical examples of how Clairvoyance has provided accurate and useful information in the past.

Teach others to recognize non-verbal cues and energies which can help them relate to the concept of Clairvoyance.

Present Clairvoyant insights in a way that is relevant to real-world issues or decisions.

Cultivating a Supportive Environment for Clairvoyants:

Offer explanations about what Clairvoyance is and what it is not, dispelling myths and misconceptions.

Respect personal boundaries when sharing Clairvoyant insights. Getting their consent is key.

It's healthy to encourage skepticism and critical thinking with Clairvoyance. Remember that everyone has their way of understanding things, and there's no need to convince anyone of anything. Just let the information come through and use it wisely with people who are eager and open to seeing beyond their current experiences. If people aren't open to you, accept that they aren't ready to hear your insight and move on.

Collaborative Engagement with Clairvoyant:

Use Clairvoyance as a tool for team problem-solving, adding insights into brainstorming sessions. Invite the Clairvoyants to contribute to or join creative projects, where their unique perspective can be particularly valuable.

Make sure that Clairvoyant abilities are used ethically and with consideration for others' privacy and well-being.

Recognizing and communicating with Clairvoyant individuals requires sensitivity and openness. By fostering understanding and respect, these sensory superpower abilities can be integrated into relationships and teams for mutual growth and enrichment.

These kinds of business partnerships can boost the team's success, increase sales, and create endless possibilities for research and development. They also are crucial in navigating tough conversations in the workplace by paying attention to non-verbal cues and adjusting your approach to connect better with others.

Practical Exercises for Clairvoyants

Developing Clairvoyance means enhancing your ability to see and understand visual information that is not physically present. Here are some practical exercises designed to refine your Clairvoyant abilities:

Sensory Recall Practice: Pick some familiar visual scenes or objects and observe them one by one. After viewing each item, take a break from any visual stimuli, then try to recall and re-experience the scene or object. This exercise boosts your memory for visuals and strengthens your ability to recall specific images without direct physical cues.

Concentrated Visualization Meditation: Choose an image or symbol to focus on, such as a flower, a star, or a landscape. Close your eyes, clear your mind, and try to visualize this image in detail without actually seeing it. This meditation enhances your focus and ability to generate detailed visual perceptions in your mind.

Blindfold Visualization: With the help of a friend, do exercises where you are blindfolded and asked to describe scenes, objects, or colors that your friend is thinking of or describing. Try to visualize these elements based solely on your intuitive perceptions without visual cues. This sharpens your mind's eye and enhances your ability to discern subtle details.

Symbol-to-Image Transformation: Focus on simple symbols, such as a circle, triangle, or square, and try to transform them, into more complex images in your mind. For example, imagine a triangle turning into a mountain or a square turning into a house. This practice helps bridge the connection between simple visual symbols and complex images, improving your seeing abilities.

Journaling Visual Experiences: Keep a journal of the visual images and scenes you perceive throughout the day, both physical and those seen through Clairvoyance. Note any emotions or physical sensations associated with these visuals. Journaling helps you document and make sense of the Clairvoyant experiences, aiding in recognizing patterns or triggers.

Progressive Relaxation for Enhanced Sensitivity: Engage in progressive muscle relaxation techniques while focusing on relaxing the eyes, forehead, and temples. Relaxing these areas can heighten sensitivity to visual stimuli, allowing for clearer and more pronounced Clairvoyant experiences.

Image Pairing Visualization: Visualize combinations of objects and their interactions before observing or creating them. Imagine how different elements combine and influence each other. This promotes creativity in visual synthesis and enhances predictive Clairvoyant abilities.

Ethical Practice Reflections: Reflect regularly on the ethical implications of your Clairvoyant experiences, especially regarding privacy and personal boundaries. This helps maintain ethical practices in using Clairvoyance, ensuring respect for others.

These exercises not only enhance Clairvoyant abilities but also foster a deeper appreciation and understanding of how these unique sensory experiences can be integrated into daily life and personal growth.

Progressive Training for Clairvoyance

Each exercise in this chapter builds upon the previous one, starting from simple visualizations to complex guided meditations that encourage deeper intuitive development. Regular practice will enhance not only your Clairvoyant capabilities but also your overall spiritual awareness. The goal is to not just see beyond the physical but to connect with and understand the deeper layers of information that Clairvoyance can reveal. This training will prepare you for more advanced Clairvoyant work, including remote viewing and other supernatural practices.

By dedicating time to these exercises and meditations, you lay a strong foundation for your Clairvoyant journey, paving the way for profound insights and enhanced intuitive capabilities. Remember, patience and consistency are key to unlocking the full potential of your superpower vision.

As you explore Clairvoyance, remember that this extraordinary ability is a tool to enhance your understanding and connection with the world around you. By honing your skills, practicing discernment, and maintaining ethical boundaries, you can transform your intuitive visions into a powerful force for good in your life and the lives of others. Embrace your abilities with gratitude and responsibility, knowing that with great power comes great potential for insight and transformation.

As we move forward to explore the next Clair-Sense, let the clarity of your visions guide you toward a future filled with wisdom, growth, and enlightened experiences. Your journey into the unseen has just begun, and the possibilities are as boundless as your imagination.

Thank you for taking this step with me. Let's continue unlocking the mysteries of your inner senses together. In the next chapter, we will be exploring Clairaudience. Let's go!

CHAPTER 3:
EMBRACING CLAIRAUDIENCE
The Symphony Of The Unheard

Welcome to the mysterious world of Clairaudience, where the unheard becomes clear, allowing you to tap into subtle whispers and frequencies of the universe. In this chapter, we'll explore how Clairaudience, can deepen your understanding, not just through sounds you hear now, but also through messages that travel through time and space.

Clairaudience, or "clear hearing," is the ability to hear things beyond normal human perception. This can include hearing spiritual guides, the thoughts of others, or sounds from different times or dimensions. Unlike ordinary hearing, this clear-hearing often involves perceiving sounds or words that provide you with guidance, warnings, or insights that others can't hear.

You might recognize that Clairaudience begins by identifying certain signs. Maybe you hear your name called when no one is around, or you get answers to questions as if someone whispered them in your ear. These experiences are not your imagination but are instead private messages meant for you. Early signs might also include a heightened sensitivity to sounds or a frequent ringing in the ears, often dismissed as tinnitus, which can be a sign of tuning into this ability.

In everyday life, Clairaudience can be very useful. It allows for deeper communication and understanding in personal and professional relationships. For example, you can sense the true feelings or intentions behind someone's words, helping you respond more effectively. This can be especially helpful in meetings or negotiations.

Developing your Clairaudience involves a mix of focus, meditation, and practice. Start by paying attention to the sounds around you—both the obvious and subtle. Meditation can help quiet your mind, making it easier to hear and, therefore, perceive and interpret the spiritual or nonphysical that are usually drowned out by daily noise. Practice listening deeply during conversations to tune into not just what is said, but what is left unsaid.

As your Clairaudient abilities grow, you may find yourself able to communicate with spiritual entities or loved ones who have passed on. This Clair-sense can provide comfort, guidance, and proof of life beyond the physical world.

This Clair offers great insights when making decisions. By listening to these higher frequencies, you can gain clarity and foresight, helping you make choices that are aligned with your highest good. This guidance is especially valuable in times of uncertainty or when you are at a crossroads in life.

It opens a gateway to a deeper understanding of the universe and your place in it. By learning to hear the subtle, and often overlooked, frequencies of life, you gain knowledge that transcends the limitations of your physical reality. This chapter invites you to tune in to this divine network of information, enriching your life with wisdom that the ears alone can hear.

This chapter aims to provide a comprehensive understanding of Clairaudience, from recognizing its signs to using its insights in everyday life. By embracing the symphony of the unheard, you can experience life with an enriched perspective, grounded in both the seen and the unseen realms.

Here is an Overview of the History of Clairaudience

The concept of Clairaudience has deep historical roots across various cultures and spiritual traditions. It is part of a broader spectrum of psychic phenomena that have been recognized and documented for centuries.

In ancient times civilizations, Clairaudience, and other sensory abilities were often linked to divine or supernatural forces. Many cultures believed that gods, spirits, or ancestral voices communicated with priests, shamans, oracles, and seers through auditory messages. For example, in ancient Greece, the Oracle of Delphi is one of the most famous examples, where the Pythia (priestess) reportedly received messages from the god Apollo. Shamans across various indigenous cultures have claimed to hear the voices of spirit guides or animal totems during rituals and healing ceremonies.

During the Middle Ages and the Renaissance, Clairaudience was viewed through the lens of religion and mysticism. One Christian mystic is Saint Hildegard of Bingen. She was a Benedictine abbess, writer, composer, and philosopher who reported experiencing visions and hearing divine voices from a young age. Hildegard claimed these voices instructed her to write down her visions, which later became significant theological works. Her experiences played a crucial role in her spiritual and intellectual contributions to Christian mysticism.

In the Kabbalah, there are accounts of mystics receiving divine revelations through auditory experiences.

The 19th century saw a surge of interest in psychic phenomena with the rise of Spiritualism, which began in the United States and spread to Europe.

Mediums often claimed to hear the voices of the deceased during séances or sessions with others, delivering messages to the living. This was seen as evidence of the afterlife and became a cornerstone of Spiritualist beliefs.

In the 20th century, parapsychology researchers began studying Clairaudience and other psychic phenomena under more scientific conditions. Institutions like the Society for Psychical Research in the UK and the Parapsychological Association in the USA conducted experiments to validate and understand Clairaudience.

Individuals like Edgar Cayce and Jane Roberts (who channeled Seth) brought Clairaudience and channeling into public awareness through their extensive work and public sessions.

Today, Clairaudience is recognized within New Age and spiritual communities as a form of psychic intuition. It is often a huge part of personal spiritual development, some meditation practices, and psychic or spiritual training workshops.

Modern practices such as yoga, meditation, and Reiki often incorporate awareness of Clairaudience as part of a broader spiritual awakening.

Researchers in fields like anomalistic psychology and neurotheology use modern technology to explore how the brain processes these experiences intending to distinguish between psychic phenomena and psychological or neurological conditions.

Throughout history, Clairaudience has been perceived and interpreted through various lenses—religious, mystical, psychological, and scientific. Each era and culture has contributed to our understanding of this phenomenon, reflecting the complex and multifaceted nature of the human and spiritual experience.

Famous Historical Figure with Clairaudience

One of the most famous historical figures known for Clairaudience is Joan of Arc. She stands out not only for her military leadership during the Hundred Years' War between France and England but also for her profound spiritual experiences, which she claimed included hearing divine voices.

Joan of Arc began hearing voices around the age of 13. She claimed that these voices were from Saint Michael, Saint Catherine, and Saint Margaret. According to Joan, the voices were sent by God and provided guidance, comfort, and instructions for her role in leading France against the English and in support of Charles VII's claim to the French throne.

The voices Joan heard played a crucial role in her decisions during military campaigns. She attributed her success at lifting the siege of Orléans and subsequent victories to the directives and intel she received from these spiritual communications with Clairaudience.

During her trial for heresy and witchcraft, Joan's Clairaudient experiences were a focal point. She defended her actions by expressing that she was merely following divine commands received through the voices of the saints. Despite her conviction and subsequent execution at the stake, her faith in the voices never wavered.

Joan of Arc's Clairaudience and her steadfast belief in her spiritual experiences have made her a legendary figure in history and a Saint in the Roman Catholic Church. Her life continues to be a subject of fascination and inspiration, reflecting the complex interplay between spirituality, leadership, and destiny.

Where is it located?

Clairaudience is a unique ability that involves both physical and spiritual listening. This extraordinary skill connects the physical world with the nonphysical, allowing you to hear sounds and receive messages beyond ordinary perception.

Interestingly, this ability is not located within the ears themselves but just behind the ears, on the bone. This specific area is energetically linked to the throat chakra, located at the base of the neck. The throat chakra serves as a crucial link between thought and expression. This connection integrates the physical act of hearing with deeper spiritual listening.

When you tap into this area behind your ears, you can perceive transcendent sounds and messages, tuning into frequencies beyond normal hearing. This remarkable ability allows you to navigate both the seen and unseen worlds, understanding and interpreting messages that transcend ordinary auditory capabilities. Through this integration, Clairaudients can decode profound information conveyed through sounds and silences, enriching their connection to the universe.

While discussing the nuances of Clairaudience with my speaking coach Monique—a double Grammy-nominated opera singer—we delved into where this sense is specifically located. As I explained its position just behind the ears, she was moved to tears, sharing that before every performance on the world stage, she instinctively rubbed those very bones, unknowingly activating her Clairaudient sense. This innate practice highlights how deeply interconnected the physical and spiritual aspects of hearing are, even in professional settings where clear communication and expression are crucial.

Through this energetic vortex behind the ears and the throat chakra, Clairaudients perceive vibrations and translate them into comprehensible messages, tuning into frequencies beyond normal hearing. In this unique confluence of the physical and the ethereal, Clairaudience resides, providing not just auditory perception but a deeper discernment and understanding of the information conveyed through sounds and silences, both heard and sensed. Through this integration, Clairaudients are equipped to navigate both the seen and the unseen worlds, decoding messages that transcend ordinary auditory capabilities.

Common Beginnings of Clairaudience

1. **Spontaneous Messages:** Many Clairaudients report hearing voices, music, or sounds that manifest spontaneously. This phenomenon can occur during both waking states and in dreams. Examples include hearing your name called with no one present, snippets of music from an unidentifiable source, or hearing conversations that are not taking place in the physical environment.

2. **Peripheral Auditory Phenomena:** You might experience clear-hearing phenomena that seem to

originate from the periphery of your environment. This could involve hearing whispers, faint murmurs, or distant echoes that vanish when focused on directly. Such experiences can be confusing initially, which could lead you to doubt your sanity, but they are authentic signs of Clairaudient's ability.

3. **Childhood Experiences:** Like Clairvoyants, Clairaudients often first notice their abilities at a young age, frequently dismissing them as figments of their imagination. Reports from children may include hearing voices that no adult can hear or possessing knowledge about events or secrets they were never told, often attributed to communications from unseen entities.

4. **Heightened Sensitivity:** Clairaudient skills often exhibit a heightened sensitivity to the sounds and vibrations around them. This heightened awareness may extend to detecting subtle changes in tone, the emotional undertones of speech, or even the silent pauses within conversations, allowing you to "hear" what isn't explicitly said.

5. **Trigger Events:** These abilities may also emerge following significant life events. Traumatic experiences such as near-death experiences, serious illnesses, or

profound emotional losses can trigger a profound shift in perception, enhancing the auditory senses to perceive beyond the normal scope of hearing.

6. **Echoes from Nature**: Often, Clairaudients find that their abilities are triggered or enhanced by natural sounds. The rustling of leaves, the sound of water flowing, or the distinct calls of birds might initiate or deepen the hearing experience, providing a connection to the natural world that transcends ordinary hearing.

7. **Technological Triggers:** Interestingly, some report that certain electronic frequencies or the buzz of modern devices can stimulate Clairaudient signs. This might include hearing indistinct voices through static noise or electronic devices triggering an unexpected Clairaudient sensation.

8. **Meditative and Spiritual Practices:** Meditating regularly, prayer, or spiritual rituals can significantly enhance Clairaudient abilities. These practices help quiet the mind and make it more receptive to subtle auditory signals, often drowned out in the busyness of everyday life. Deep meditative states are particularly conducive to opening the auditory channels to the spiritual realm.

9. **Cultural and Ritualistic Practices:** In some cultures, ritualistic practices involving drumming, chanting, or other rhythmic sound use can awaken or amplify Clairaudient abilities. These rituals often create an auditory pathway to trance-like states where their clear-hearing is heightened.

10. **Amplified Perception in Social Settings:** Clairaudients may find that they hear and assimilate information in social settings, such as meetings, that others do not comprehend. This heightened awareness allows you to perceive underlying messages or subtle innuendoes in conversations, detect discrepancies between spoken words and true intentions, or even hear whispered discussions from across the room. This capacity can provide significant insights into the dynamics and decision-making processes, often giving Clairaudients an advantage because of your deeper understanding of the context and the words being expressed, which can be beneficial in professional and personal interactions.

11. **Sudden Discomfort in Noisy Environments:** For some of you, who haven't yet learned to manage your sensitivity or control your hearing ability, you might feel the need to avoid large gatherings or feel overwhelmed

by too much noise. This happens because your sensory superpower picks up sounds and the energy of people around you and often, this can feel too intense. This is because you don't just hear the sounds, but also sense the emotions and energy of everyone around them.

By understanding these common beginnings, you may better recognize and nurture your Clairaudient abilities, integrating them into your daily life or spiritual practices for deeper personal growth and understanding.

Signs of Emerging Clairaudience

1. **Hearing Sounds That Aren't There:** Sometimes, you might hear sounds, voices, or music that others can't hear. This could be like hearing someone call your name when no one is around or catching bits of music or conversations that don't seem to come from anywhere.
2. **Hearing Auras:** Some Clairaudients can hear the energy fields around people. This might start as a soft hum or vibration and can develop into specific sounds or musical tones linked to someone's aura.
3. **Hearing the Future:** This means receiving information about future events through voices or sounds. You might hear a conversation before it

happens or get a warning about something that's going to happen.

4. **Hearing Spirits or Entities:** This involves communicating with non-physical beings. Clairaudients might hear the voices of loved ones who have passed away or spiritual guides offering advice or comfort.

5. **Intuitive Listening:** This is when you suddenly understand deeper truths about situations or people through what you hear. It could be overhearing part of a conversation that answers a question you have or picking up on the true feelings behind someone's words.

Recognizing and accepting these signs can be your first step toward embracing your Clairaudient abilities. By developing them further, you can enhance your spiritual communication and hearing superpowers. This gives you an advantage in connecting with others in both your personal and professional lives. Imagine being able to understand people better and picking up on things that most people miss. This can help you build stronger relationships, solve problems more effectively, and even stand out in your career. So, don't be afraid to explore and develop your Clairaudient skills – they could be the key to unlocking new opportunities and deeper connections.

Signs you have Clairaudience

Symptoms or signs of Clairaudience will vary but typically include the following experiences which indicate a heightened intuitive ability to receive insight while hearing beyond what is normally experienced:

1. **Hearing Voices or Sounds:** You might hear sounds, voices, music or even your name called faintly without it happening in your current reality.
2. **Knowing the Future:** Sometimes you might hear things about future events before they happen, like a voice warning you about something.
3. **Telepathic Hearing:** This is hearing someone's thoughts or a conversation even if you're not close to them. It can also mean you hear what someone is thinking before they say it out loud. This can be tricky because you hear it twice: once in their thoughts and then again when they speak it aloud.
4. **Hearing Energy:** You can hear the sounds or vibrations around people, animals, or objects that others can't hear.
5. **Talking to Spirits:** You might hear spiritual beings, guides, or angels that aren't visible to others.

6. **Symbolic Sounds:** In your dreams, you might hear sounds or music that have special messages or predict the future.
7. **Faint Noises:** Sometimes, you might hear faint whispers or noises that seem to come from nowhere.
8. **Ear Sensations:** You might feel tingling, warmth, or pressure around your ears, which is connected to your ability to hear these special sounds.
9. **Sudden Insights:** You get clear ideas or solutions to problems out of nowhere, like a sudden flash of understanding.
10. **Noticing Patterns:** You hear patterns or sequences in sounds that seem to carry important messages.
11. **Hearing Something Again:** You might feel like you've heard a specific sound or conversation before, even if you haven't. It feels familiar somehow. Or, when someone thinks something, you may hear the thought, before they speak it. Therefore, when they do speak, it is the second time you've heard the words.
12. **Vivid Dreams:** Your dreams have very clear and realistic sounds that provide important information.
13. **Psychic Echoes:** You hear echoes or remnants of sounds that help you understand situations or people better.

14. **Intuitive Listening:** You develop a keen sense of what people really mean, beyond just their words.
15. **Clear Soundscapes:** You encounter very clear and memorable auditory experiences, especially in dreams, that carry significant messages.
16. **Ear Buzzing:** Sometimes you might feel a buzzing or pulsing in your ears, connected to hearing special sounds.
17. **Natural Affinity:** You naturally enjoy auditory activities like music or sound healing.
18. **Instant Understanding:** You suddenly understand complex ideas or emotions from others through subtle sounds or changes in tone.
19. **Accurate Predictions:** You hear things about future events or emotional shifts that turn out to be true.
20. **Symbolic Language:** You intuitively understand the symbolic meanings of sounds or spoken words that appear in your mind or dreams.
21. **Receiving Guidance:** It feels like specific advice or warnings are directly communicated to you through sound.
22. **Sensitive to Environment:** You're very aware of changes in sound or sudden silences in your surroundings.

23. **Auditory Coincidences:** You often hear coincidental sounds that seem to guide or inform your decisions.
24. **Echo Affirmations:** You receive confirmations from the environment through sounds, like hearing relevant phrases or names that respond to your thoughts or questions.

These signs of Clairaudience can be very personal and vary in how often they happen. Many people with these abilities develop them further through meditation, intuitive exercises, and learning from experts to harness and refine their skills.

Real Examples of Clairaudience

One evening, I was being taught to hear beyond words. I had been studying this for a while when I was guided to read the book Ask and It is Given by Esther and Jerry Hicks. To me, what I was asked to do while the TV was playing with my husband in the room watching a movie was confusing. I was guided to take a big pause after reading one word and was being taught to hear between the words. I didn't understand and questioned this with, "Are you sure you know what you are doing? Why would I read one word and then pause, before going to the next word in the book?"

I heard a resounding "Yes, please do this exercise and see what happens".

As I paused after the first word, nothing happened. I did it again after the second word, I began to realize that there was much more going on in the nonphysical than I thought, and I began to hear my guides having conversations. For a moment, I thought I was going crazy because I was hearing what was going on in the room with the TV, was reading this book, and now began to hear the conversations about what I was doing and how important it was, as if I was spying on my "team" as I call them, my guides/angels. When I tapped into this clear-hearing and clear-seeing, they turned and faced me and smiled and said, "There she is, she's done it, she hears and sees us!"

I began to hear the ringing of phones, the ringing of a doorbell, and conversations going on, and realized that the ability to hear can transcend time-space reality and that I was experiencing what I call blurred lines, between this reality and another where others were occupying the same space according to Quantum Physics.

One of the things that I teach my clients in developing their Clairaudient abilities is to listen to their heart and what their true self has to say about something. Very often, in sessions, I ask people questions and when they answer, I will say, "Sweetheart, that's not what I heard your spirit say, would you like to try that again?" They take a deep breath, as they know to do, sometimes touching their heart and then they hear what the truth is, and not what they perceive the truth to be. It's always so much deeper than they think their thoughts are, and this helps them to develop their clear-hearing abilities and tap into their innate knowing and intelligence that can guide them to the truth, where they are set free.

One day, I was asking a client of mine what his life was like. His immediate response was that his life was great. When I asked him to dig deeper, it took him a little while to "get off of the chalkboard", as I call it, trying to figure out the equations without tapping into his hearing abilities. He has learned to back away from the board with promptings and to tap into the heart and hear what thoughts he's had lately about his life.

Instead of the peace and great life he was trying to convince himself and thus me, that he was having, he found out the following:

- He was trying to make playing small okay.

- He didn't like feeling that he had to walk on eggshells because he was living in an apartment and didn't want others to hear him.
- He realized he didn't like the area in which he lived.
- He didn't like how small his apartment was.
- He didn't like how small the bathroom was.
- He realized that he wanted an island in the kitchen.

The mind is a very interesting thing and hearing your inner thoughts equates to developing your Clairaudient abilities. Once he realized that he was thinking these things with me helping him by hearing through his hearing sensory superpower, what his real wants and needs were, he began to realize that he was convincing himself to stay put and wait, that it wasn't that bad, and now understands that he was in scarcity thinking and wanted more.

He left the session placing his order for a new space and a newfound ability to hear what he really thinks about his life and what he wants and deserves.

Benefits of Hearing in Communication

In Relationships:

Clairaudience can greatly enhance your ability to communicate and connect with others. It allows you to pick up on tones, emotions, and even unspoken thoughts, giving you a unique edge in all relationships. This extra intuitive information helps you understand and respond to others in ways that those without this ability cannot.

A Clairaudient can sense the feelings and intentions behind words. This helps you respond with kindness and understanding, deepening the bond and connections with others.

By hearing unspoken feelings or potential misunderstandings, you can address issues before they become bigger problems. This helps keep relationships more supportive and nurturing, and can greatly increase your sales in business.

In Monetizing:

Clairaudience can be very valuable in the business world. It helps you make smart decisions by giving you insights into conversations, team dynamics, and competitive moves that others might miss.

Clairaudients can offer their abilities to guide people or businesses in making important decisions. This makes you a valuable consultant because of the insights you hear and interpret.

By hearing the unspoken thoughts, you can navigate negotiations with better foresight, leading to better outcomes and financial gains.

Getting Clarity on Others:

Discerning the true intentions and integrity of others can safeguard against deception, ensuring trust in personal and professional relationships.

By understanding the needs and preferences of another person, you can tailor your communication to be more effective and appreciated. This helps you reach people on a deeper level, making people more likely to want to be around you and work with you.

Cultivating Clairaudience for Growth:

Regularly practicing mindfulness and listening exercises can enhance your Clairaudience. This helps you hear more clearly and accurately.

Sharing insights with others and getting feedback can refine the ability to interpret what you hear.

Engaging with books and courses on Clairaudience can provide tools and techniques to better use this ability.

Expanding Clairaudient Abilities:

Regularly do exercises that improve your listening skills and your ability to interpret sounds. When you walk away from a conversation, recount precisely what your takeaway was.

Doing sound meditations, such as focusing on different frequencies or tones, can increase your sensitivity to your hearing superpowers.

Being a part of groups or communities that focus on psychic development can offer support and shared experiences, helping you grow faster.

By incorporating these practices, Clairaudience can not only improve personal relationships but also open avenues for professional growth and financial opportunities.

Potential Challenges of Clairaudience if Mismanaged or Unrecognized

Having Clairaudience can bring a unique set of challenges and issues for those who possess or develop these abilities. Here are some potential issues that Clairaudients may face:

1. **Overload:** Constant or intense Clairaudient information can be overwhelming, leading to mental

exhaustion. This may make it hard to filter out background noises, causing distraction or irritation.
2. **Confusion:** It can be challenging to tell the difference between sounds from the spiritual realm and those in the physical world, which can be disorienting.
3. **Emotional Impact:** Hearing voices associated with negative experiences or emotions can lead to anxiety or fear.
4. **Privacy Issues:** Clairaudients might accidentally hear private conversations or thoughts not meant for them.
5. **Misinterpretation:** There's a risk of misinterpreting Clairaudient messages, which can result in wrong decisions or spreading misinformation.
6. **Skepticism:** Encountering disbelief from others can lead to feelings of isolation or self-doubt.
7. **Social Stigma:** Psychic abilities can carry a social stigma, affecting personal and professional relationships and possibly leading to isolation.
8. **Mental Health Concerns:** Clairaudients may question their mental health, fearing they might be labeled as delusional or mentally unstable.
9. **Physical Symptoms:** Some individuals report tinnitus or headaches when their abilities become active.

10. **Understanding:** Friends and family might struggle to understand or accept the Clairaudient's experiences, complicating relationships.
11. **Emotional Boundaries:** Clairaudients may find it difficult to separate their feelings from the emotions they hear from others, leading to emotional entanglement.
12. **Responsibility:** Handling Clairaudient information comes with ethical considerations about when and how to share it.
13. **Distraction:** Focusing on auditory messages can sometimes distract from living in the present and handling immediate tasks.
14. **Expectations:** Others might have unrealistic expectations of Clairaudient's abilities, assuming they are infallible, which can lead to pressure and stress.
15. **Seclusion:** Clairaudients might want to avoid social gatherings and noise to manage overwhelming auditory input and find peace.
16. **Assimilation:** They may struggle with hearing too many things at once and not knowing how to process that information. Ambient noises can be particularly challenging.

Clairaudients often benefit from learning how to manage their abilities and finding a balance to address these challenges. This can involve setting healthy boundaries, developing coping strategies, and seeking support from understanding communities. It's important to get guidance from a highly developed Clairaudient who can teach them about their abilities clearly and cohesively to help them succeed.

Career Paths for Clairaudients

Counseling and Therapy: They can thrive in psychology and counseling because they can hear beyond words. This ability helps them understand clients' unspoken feelings and thoughts, which is crucial for addressing deeper emotional and psychological issues. This makes them effective therapists, counselors, or life coaches.

Music Industry Professionals: Clairaudients have heightened auditory sensitivity, making them naturally suited for music careers. They can work as performers, composers, sound engineers, or producers, perceiving nuances in sound that others might miss, which enriches music creation and production.

Creative Writing and Journalism: Clear-hearers often have a talent for "hearing" the voices of characters or the essence of a story. This makes them skilled writers and journalists, capable of conveying deeper truths and insights through their narratives.

Mediation and Conflict Resolution: Having these abilities can make excellent mediators because they can hear what is not said. They can work in legal settings, human resources, or as independent consultants, helping to resolve disputes by clarifying misunderstandings and facilitating effective communication.

Spiritual Leadership or Mentoring: Many Clairaudients feel a strong connection to spiritual realms, leading to roles in spiritual leadership. They can work as pastors, spiritual mentors, or leaders of workshops and retreats focused on psychic development and spiritual growth.

Teaching and Education: Often, having this sensory superpower can be an effective educators, especially in subjects involving listening and oral skills. They can teach languages, music, or any subject where their auditory abilities enhance the learning experience.

Sound Therapy and Healing: Clear-hearers can use their understanding of sound to practice sound healing. They might use tools like tuning forks, singing bowls, or musical compositions to promote healing and well-being.

Law Enforcement and Investigative Roles: They may find fulfilling careers in law enforcement or private investigation. Their ability to pick up on auditory clues that others overlook can be crucial in solving cases.

Customer Service and Support: You'll find that they excel in customer service roles that require active listening. They can truly hear and address customer concerns, often preempting issues before they escalate.

Voice Acting, Performing, and Public Speaking: Having these abilities can be great careers for vocal talents and sensitivity to audience reactions in careers like voice acting, singing, acting, and public speaking. Their ability to engage and resonate with large audiences collectively is a benefit.

Audio Engineering and Technical Production: People with these abilities are well-suited to sound editing, mixing, and production roles. Their acute hearing helps them detect subtle audio issues, leading to careers in film, television, radio, and live performances.

Entrepreneurship in Audio and Communication Technologies: People who pursue business careers might develop innovative audio devices, communication tools, or educational platforms that utilize sound uniquely.

In these varied careers, Clairaudients can leverage their unique auditory capabilities to enhance their professional effectiveness and contribute meaningfully to their fields, benefiting both themselves and their communities.

Detecting Clairaudience in Others

Recognizing Clairaudient abilities in others allows for deeper interaction and understanding. Here's how you might detect Clairaudience:

Observational Signs:

A person might respond to questions or comments that have not been spoken aloud, indicating they've heard thoughts or unvoiced remarks.

They may appear to be listening to something that isn't audibly present or reacting to sounds that others cannot hear.

Notice if they often seem to respond to sounds or whispers that are not apparent to others, as if catching something on the edge of their auditory perception.

Behavioral Indicators:

They may speak of hearing things before they happen, such as mentioning a song just before it plays on the radio or reacting to a statement before it's made. Or, even singing a song in the morning, and then out in public, they hear it playing. It's like they heard it before they were exposed to it in person.

A strong reaction to the tone or emotion in someone's voice, even when the spoken words are neutral, can indicate Clairaudient sensitivity.

They might discuss hearing distinct voices or sounds in their dreams that later manifest, or share insights gained from dream conversations. It's as if they were meeting with someone in the ethereal and then relaying it to you.

Communicating with a Clairaudient Individual:

Be clear and straightforward in your communications. Clairaudients may pick up on the emotional undertones of your words or the thoughts behind them.

Engaging in discussions about metaphysical topics can create a supportive environment for them to share their hearing sensitivities.

Validate their experiences without judgment, which can encourage open and honest communication about their hearing insights.

By understanding these signs, you can better interact with people who have Clairaudient abilities, building a relationship that benefits from a deep mutual understanding and respect.

Cultivating a Supportive Environment for Clairaudients:

Offer explanations about what Clairaudience is and what it is not, dispelling myths and misconceptions.

Respect personal boundaries when sharing your insights. Getting someone's permission to speak about these things is key to respecting others.

It's healthy to encourage skepticism and critical thinking, allowing for a balanced perspective on clear-hearing messages. Just remember that they are not getting the information you are, so patience is key here.

Use your ability to hear the sounds and beyond the sounds, as a tool for collaborative problem-solving, inciting conversations to brainstorm more effectively.

Invite the Clairaudient individual to contribute to creative projects, where their unique clear-hearing can be insightful and valuable.

Ensure that these abilities are used ethically and with consideration for their and other's privacy and well-being.

Recognizing and communicating with people who have Clairaudient abilities requires being sensitive and open-minded. By understanding and respecting their skills, you can build stronger relationships and more effective teams. These abilities can boost team success, increase sales, and open endless possibilities for research and development. These clear-hearers can also help navigate tough conversations at work by paying close attention to what the other person is saying and adjusting their responses to bring unity into the workplace.

Leveraging Clairaudience Collaboratively:

Hiring clairaudients is a powerful and strategic tool in group problem-solving, adding these special insights to improve brainstorming and decision-making.

Take advantage of their unique hearing abilities to boost creative projects. Their special way of perceiving sounds can add new ideas and depth, making their input super valuable in artistic or creative tasks.

Make sure Clairaudient abilities are used ethically, respecting everyone's privacy and feelings.

Interacting with people with this sensory superpower requires a lot of empathy and openness. By creating a respectful and understanding environment, Clairaudient skills can fit smoothly into both work and personal life. This helps team dynamics and encourages mutual growth. Such approaches can make teams more effective, spark innovation, and open new possibilities for research and development. Plus, this can be beneficial in handling tricky conversations at work, offering a deeper grasp of hidden messages and emotions that might otherwise be missed.

Practical Exercises for Clairaudients

Developing Clairaudience involves sharpening your ability to hear and interpret subtle sounds that aren't physically present. Here are some practical exercises to help you improve your Clairaudient abilities:

Sensory Recall Practice: Listen to a variety of familiar sounds one by one. After hearing each sound, spend some time in silence and try to mentally recall and re-experience the sound. This helps improve your memory for sounds and strengthens your ability to recall auditory details without hearing them again.

Concentrated Sound Meditation: Choose a sound to focus on, like a bell, a stream, or the sounds of the ocean or water. Close your eyes, clear your mind, and try to imagine the sound in your head without actually hearing it. This meditation helps you focus and generate detailed auditory perceptions internally, enhancing your Clairaudient skills.

Blind Listening Tests: With the help of a friend, conduct blind listening tests using different sounds. Try to identify the sounds based only on what you hear without visual clues. This practice sharpens your hearing and helps you notice subtle differences and details in sounds.

Sound-to-Emotion Transformation: Listen to different pieces of music, tones, or natural sounds and try to convert these auditory stimuli into emotional experiences. This helps you connect auditory perception with emotional responses, improving your overall sensory integration.

Journaling Auditory Experiences: Keep a journal of the sounds you experience each day, both physical and those perceived through Clairaudience. Note any emotional or physical sensations associated with these sounds. Journaling helps document and make sense of your Clairaudient experiences, helping you recognize patterns or triggers.

Progressive Relaxation for Enhanced Sensitivity: Practice progressive muscle relaxation techniques while focusing on relaxing your ears, jaw, and neck specifically. Relaxing these areas can heighten your sensitivity to sounds, leading to clearer and more pronounced Clairaudient experiences.

Sound Pairing Visualization: Visualize how different sounds interact with each other before actually hearing them. Imagine how various sounds combine and affect each other. This practice promotes creativity in sound synthesis and enhances your predictive Clairaudient abilities.

Ethical Practice Reflections: Regularly reflect on the ethical implications of your Clairaudient experiences, especially concerning privacy and personal boundaries. This helps ensure you maintain ethical practices when using Clairaudience, respecting others' boundaries and personal integrity.

These exercises not only improve your Clairaudient abilities but also help you appreciate and understand how these unique sensory experiences can be integrated into your daily life and personal growth.

Progressive Training

Each exercise in this chapter builds upon the previous one, starting from simple sound awareness to guided auditory meditations that encourage deeper psychic development. By regularly practicing these exercises, you'll not only improve your Clairaudient abilities but also enhance your overall spiritual awareness. The goal is to hear beyond the physical and connect with the deeper layers of information that Clairaudience can reveal. This progressive training will prepare you for more advanced Clairaudient work, including receiving guidance from higher realms and other psychic practices.

By dedicating time to these exercises and meditations, you create a strong foundation for your Clairaudient journey, paving the way for profound insights and enhanced intuitive skills. Remember, patience and consistency are key to unlocking the full potential of your psychic hearing.

As you delve deeper into the realm of Clairaudience, keep in mind that this extraordinary gift is a tool to enhance your understanding and connection with the world around you. By honing your skills, practicing discernment, and maintaining ethical boundaries, you can transform your intuitive hearing into a powerful force for good in your life and the lives of others. Embrace your Clairaudient abilities with gratitude and responsibility, knowing that with great power comes great potential for insight and transformation.

As you move forward to explore the next Clair-Sense, let the clarity of your inner hearing guide you toward a future filled with wisdom, growth, and enlightened experiences. Your journey into the realm of unseen sounds has just begun, and the possibilities are as boundless as your imagination.

Thank you for taking this step with me. Let's continue unlocking the mysteries of your inner senses together. In the next chapter, we will be exploring Clairgustance. Let's go!

CHAPTER 4:
THE FLAVOR OF INSIGHT
Unlocking The Power of Clairgustance

Welcome to the tantalizing world of Clairgustance, where you can taste flavors of the seen and unseen, allowing you to savor the subtle essences and divine message of the universe. This chapter explores the amazing ability of clear-tasting and shows how this sensory ability helps you understand not just through the physical taste of the present but also connects you to the profound messages that travel through time and space.

Clairgustance, or "clear tasting," is the sense that gives you the ability to taste and discern flavors beyond the normal scope of tasting. This can include tasting the essence of spiritual entities, the emotional residue of others, or even the distinct flavors of different dimensions. Unlike ordinary tasting, this sensory superpower often involves perceiving tastes that provide guidance, warnings, or insights that others can't.

Recognizing your ability starts by noticing its signs. Maybe you taste something when there is no food around, or you experience flavors that correlate with specific emotions or memories. These experiences are not your imagination but are instead profound communications meant just for you. Early signs might also include a heightened sensitivity to flavors or a strange aftertaste, often overlooked as mere imagination, which serves as a tuning mechanism for this sense.

In everyday life, using this sensory superpower can be incredibly beneficial. It allows you to empathize and understand personal and professional relationships. For instance, by tasting the essence behind someone's words, you can detect the true intentions or feelings behind them. In meetings or negotiations, this can guide you to respond more effectively, aligning not just with spoken words but with unspoken truths.

Developing this superpower involves focus, meditation, and practice. Start by paying attention to the flavors around you—both obvious and subtle. Meditation helps calm the mind, making it easier to perceive and interpret the spiritual or emotional essences that are typically ignored by daily distractions. Practicing mindful eating during meals can also sharpen your skills, helping you to tune into not just the flavors of food, but also what these tastes say about their origins and your surroundings. Take time to savor the different flavors.

As your Clairgustance abilities grow, you may find yourself able to communicate with spiritual beings or connect deeply with people through the universal language of taste. This can provide comfort, guidance, and proof of life beyond the physical.

This superpower gives you deeper insights and develops your intuition when making decisions. By savoring these higher frequencies, you can gain clarity and foresight, helping you to make choices that align with your highest good. This guidance is especially valuable in times of uncertainty or when making huge changes in your life.

Clairgustance opens a gateway to a deeper understanding of the universe and your place within it. By learning to discern the subtle, and often overlooked, flavors of life, you equip yourself with the knowledge that transcends the limitations of physical reality. This chapter invites you to indulge in this divine spectrum of flavors, enriching your life with wisdom that the tongue alone could never perceive.

This chapter aims to provide a fuller understanding of Clairgustance, from recognizing its signs to using its insights in everyday life. By embracing the symphony of the unflavored experiences, you allow yourself to live with an enriched perspective, grounded in both the seen and the unseen realms.

Here is an Overview of the History of Clairgustance

The history of clear-tasting is not as well-documented as some other supernatural abilities, such as Clairvoyance or Clairaudience, but it has deep roots in various cultural and spiritual traditions around the world. Here's a look at the historical background and significance of this sensory superpower.

In many ancient cultures, eating and tasting weren't just physical actions but also spiritual experiences. Rituals often included eating foods believed to offer spiritual visions or connections to the divine. For example, the use of entheogens—substances that change perception and consciousness for religious purposes—is a form of Clairgustance. Substances like ayahuasca in South American traditions or soma in Vedic rituals were used to get spiritual messages through their flavors and the experiences they created.

During the Middle Ages and the Renaissance, the concept of tasting the divine was used in Christian mysticism. Mystics like Saint Catherine of Siena described experiencing divine communion through what could be interpreted as Clairgustance, getting spiritual insights and intuition through tastes that were supernaturally given with spiritual significance.

In various indigenous cultures, shamans and healers often used taste as a means to diagnose illnesses or communicate with the spiritual world. They might taste a substance or the air itself to get information from the spiritual realm, using their enhanced sensory abilities to guide their community or heal the sick.

With the rise of Spiritualism in the 19th century, there was a renewed interest in different forms of psychic phenomena, including clear-taste. Mediums and psychics would often claim to taste the essence of spirits or astral entities as part of their abilities, using these experiences to convey messages from the deceased or to provide evidence of life beyond death.

In contemporary spiritual and New Age circles, Clairgustance is recognized as part of a broader range of extrasensory perceptions. Practitioners may use this sense in conjunction with other psychic senses to get holistic information. It's often discussed in holistic health and spiritual healing, where practitioners might use their ability to taste the energy of a person's health or the purity of food and substances.

Modern parapsychology occasionally studies this sensory superpower within the field of anomalous cognition, although it's a less explored area compared to other psychic phenomena. Researchers might look at the neurological and psychological aspects of how some people claim to perceive taste without a physical source, considering both the psychic and ordinary explanations for such experiences.

Clairgustance, like many psychic abilities, reflects a mix of historical, cultural, and spiritual perspectives, each adding layers of understanding to this unique sensory ability. Its history shows how closely our senses are to our interpretation of spiritual and metaphysical realities.

Famous Historical Figure with Clairgustance

One of the most intriguing historical figures known for experiencing clear-tasting is Hildegard of Bingen. She was a famous mystic and spiritual leader of the 12th century, Hildegard's experiences with Clairgustance were a big part of her extensive work in medicine, music, and theology.

Hildegard of Bingen reported experiencing divine revelations not just through sights and sounds but also through the profound tastes of holy sacraments and medicinal plants, which she believed carried a deep spiritual meaning and significance. She described these tastes in her writings as "the taste of the divine", a miraculous sense that guided her in creating herbal remedies and medical practices.

These divine flavors played a crucial role in Hildegard's holistic view of health and spirituality. She utilized her Clairgustance in her medical practice, often prescribing foods and herbs that she perceived to have beneficial spiritual and physical properties. Her ability to 'taste' the quality and virtue of substances contributed to her pioneering work in nutritional healing and natural science.

During her life, Hildegard's spiritual and sensory experiences were well-documented and revered, allowing her to consult with and advise popes, emperors, and bishops. Her written works, which include descriptions of her mystical experiences and practical applications of her sensory insights, were unprecedented at the time and continue to influence herbal medicine and spiritual practices today.

Hildegard of Bingen's legacy as a Clairgustant, alongside her numerous other talents, has made her a legendary figure in both historical and spiritual contexts. Her life remains a profound testament to the unique interplay between spirituality, health, and destiny, and her experiences offer rich insights into the historical scope of Clairgustance.

Where is it located?

Clairgustance, a faculty that enables tasting transcendent flavors and messages, goes beyond the usual sense of taste by combining the physical act of tasting and deeper spiritual sensing. This amazing ability isn't located on the tongue itself but is associated with the area around the solar plexus chakra, just above the stomach. This specific area is energetically linked to personal power and emotional processing and serves as a bridge between physical taste and metaphysical insights.

Many people might not realize how closely connected the physical and spiritual aspects of taste are. For instance, some chefs, known for their intuitive cooking, may naturally place their hands over their solar plexus before creating a new dish. This instinctive action can activate their Clairgustant sense, allowing them to tune into subtle flavors and gain deeper insights into their culinary creations. Much like you heard the reference earlier of my speaking coach Monique rubbing the bones behind the ears just before she went on stage. It was an intuitive way to connect to her Clairaudient abilities.

This connection highlights how the solar plexus chakra plays a crucial role in Clairgustance, enabling individuals to perceive flavors that go beyond ordinary taste. By integrating physical tasting with spiritual sensing, clear-tasters can navigate both the seen and unseen worlds, decoding messages that transcend normal gustatory capabilities.

Through this energetic center near the solar plexus, Clairgustants perceive subtle essences and translate them into comprehensible insights, tuning into flavors beyond normal tasting. In this unique confluence of the physical and the ethereal, this sensory superpower resides, providing not just gustatory perception but a deeper discernment and understanding of the information conveyed through flavors and aromas, both tasted and sensed. Through this integration, Clairgustants are equipped to navigate both the seen and the unseen worlds, decoding messages that transcend ordinary gustatory capabilities.

Common Beginnings of Clairgustance

1. **Spontaneous Tastes:** People with Clairgustance often taste flavors without any food being present. This can happen when they're awake or even in their dreams. For example, they might taste a certain food or drink that's not there or experience flavors connected to their memories or emotions.
2. **Peripheral Taste Phenomena:** Sometimes, people taste things that seem to come from the edges of their awareness. These tastes can suddenly appear and disappear when they try to focus on them. This can be confusing at first, but it's a real part of having clear-tasting abilities.

3. **Tastes from Childhood:** Many notice their abilities when they are young but often think they are just imagining things. Kids might taste things no one else can or know about flavors they've never tried before. These experiences are often linked to unseen sources.

4. **Super Sensitive Taste:** Clairgustants often have a very keen sense of taste. They can notice slight changes in flavors or sense the emotions connected to certain foods or drinks, allowing them to "taste" things others might miss.

5. **Trigger Events:** Major life events like near-death experiences, serious illnesses, or big emotional losses can trigger Clairgustance signs. These events can change how they taste things, making their sense of taste more sensitive. It also means they can tap into things from their past that remind them of something traumatic they experienced that they have not done the inner healing work on, so the present can be triggered by these tastes.

6. **Nature's Flavors:** People with these superpowers find that their abilities are heightened by natural flavors. The taste of herbs, the earthy flavor of rain, or seasonal changes can start or enhance their experiences, connecting them to nature in a special way.

7. **Technological Triggers:** Some report that certain chemicals or modern materials can trigger Clairgustant episodes. For instance, they might taste strange flavors in city environments or when near new synthetic materials.
8. **Meditative and Spiritual Practices:** Regular meditation, prayer, or spiritual rituals can boost clear-tasting abilities. These practices help quiet the mind and make it easier to notice subtle tastes often drowned out by everyday noise. Deep meditation is especially good for opening to taste spiritual flavors.
9. **Cultural and Ritualistic Practices:** In some cultures, rituals involving specific foods, spices, or drinks can awaken or enhance Clairgustance. These rituals create a pathway to deeper states where clear tastes and messages become more accessible.
10. **Amplified Perception in Social Settings:** People who have these sensory superpowers might taste flavors in social settings, like dinners or tastings, that others don't notice. This awareness helps them understand the true flavors and emotional undertones of food, giving them deeper insights during social interactions.
11. **Sudden Clarity in Flavorful Environments:** Some Clairgustants realize their abilities when they can

clearly taste and understand flavors in complex environments. They might discern specific ingredients in a dish or taste subtle nuances others can't detect, providing insights into their surroundings and the emotions of those around them.

Understanding these common experiences can help people recognize and nurture their clear-tasting superpowers, using them for personal growth and deeper understanding.

Signs of Emerging Clairgustance

This sensory ability is also known as a special ability where people can taste things without actual food around. This superpower lets you sense flavors from a deeper spiritual or energetic level, connecting the physical world with the spiritual realm.

1. **How Clairgustance Works:** This sensory ability uses your taste buds and tongue, just like regular tasting. Normally, food molecules interact with taste receptors on your tongue, sending signals to your brain that tell you what you're tasting. With clear-tasting, though, you can taste flavors with or without food. It's

like your brain is receiving taste signals from an invisible source.

2. **Linked to the Nervous System:** If you have this sensory superpower, tasting something might feel like remembering a favorite flavor or experiencing a strong taste connected to a memory or emotion. The difference is that this can happen spontaneously, without any recent food experiences or physical triggers. This suggests that Clairgustance uses special brain pathways that skip the usual sensory methods, directly engaging the parts of the brain responsible for taste.

3. **Psychic and Spiritual Connections: Tasting from Afar:** This superpower is deeply connected to psychic and spiritual realms. People with this ability often receive messages or insights from spiritual guides, loved ones who have passed away, or a collective unconscious. These messages come through as symbolic tastes. For example, tasting honey might mean something sweet or good is coming your way, while a sour taste could be a warning.

4. **Emotional and Energy Links:** Tastes can trigger strong emotions and memories. In this sensory ability, the tastes you experience might reflect the emotional or energy states of people or places. For example, you

might taste sweetness around someone very happy or bitterness in a place with a sad history.

5. **Practical Uses:** Clear-tasting can be useful in many areas. Chefs with this ability might create amazing new dishes. Therapists could use it to understand their clients' feelings better. In spiritual practices, this superpower can help with cleansing rituals or identifying different energies or entities.

6. **Developing Clairgustance:** Like other psychic abilities, this sensory superpower can also be developed through practice and meditation. You might focus on the sensation of tasting while meditating, clear your mind to receive these subtle signals, or use crystals that enhance these abilities.

Understanding clear-tasting means you recognize its connection to both our physical senses and deeper spiritual insights. It goes beyond ordinary taste experiences, giving those with this ability a unique perspective on the world.

Clairgustance is a fascinating sensory ability that bridges the gap between the physical and spiritual worlds, allowing communication through taste. By going beyond ordinary sensory experiences, this superpower provides insights and connections, revealing hidden emotions and spiritual messages. Those who develop this sense of clear-taste can understand the world more deeply, improve their interactions with others, and gain a richer perspective on life. As we learn more about this ability, it holds the promise of deepening our connection to both the seen and unseen aspects of our existence.

Signs You Have Clairgustance

Clairgustance, or "clear tasting," as you know by now, is a special ability where people can taste things that aren't present. Here are some signs that you might have this amazing superpower.

1. **Tasting What's Not There:** You taste flavors, foods, or drinks that aren't there. You can also feel things in your throat area that feel thicker than normal which identifies that there is a taste and smell in the air.
2. **Future Flavors:** You get a taste of something that hints at an event before it happens.
3. **Tasting from Afar:** You can taste what someone else is eating or experiencing, even if you're not with them just by thinking of them.
4. **Flavor Auras:** You taste flavors or essences around people, animals, or objects that others can't.

5. **Spiritual Flavors:** You taste things connected to spiritual entities or guides that aren't visible.
6. **Dream Tastes:** You taste flavors in dreams that seem to carry messages or predict future events.
7. **Faint Tastes:** You detect faint tastes that appear from nowhere.
8. **Stomach Sensations:** You feel warmth or tingling in your stomach related to your taste ability.
9. **Sudden Insights:** You get clear taste-related insights or solutions without knowing how. How someone smells can identify their mood and if you wish to be around them.
10. **Pattern Recognition:** You notice taste patterns that seem to convey messages or warnings.
11. **Deja Taste:** You have a strong sensation of having already tasted a specific flavor or dish.
12. **Vivid Dream Tastes:** Your dreams have distinct, lifelike flavors that might tell you about future events.
13. **Psychic Tastes:** You experience leftover tastes that give you insights about situations or people.
14. **Intuitive Tasting:** You sense deeper truths in meals or food experiences beyond what's served.

15. **Flavorful Dreams:** You have exceptionally clear and memorable taste experiences in dreams that carry important messages.
16. **Energetic Stomach:** You feel fluttering or pulsing in your stomach related to your taste perception.
17. **Love for Tasting:** You naturally enjoy culinary arts, tasting, or food rituals, even if you haven't pursued them before.
18. **Sudden Understanding:** You suddenly understand complex flavors or people's emotions through taste.
19. **Accurate Predictions:** You have taste-related premonitions about events or emotional shifts that come true.
20. **Symbolic Flavors:** You understand the symbolic meanings of flavors or dishes that appear in your mind or dreams.
21. **Dietary Guidance:** You feel like you get direct taste-related advice or warnings about your diet, especially for future health. This could come across as a knowing that you shouldn't eat something you just took a bite of.
22. **Sensitive to Taste Changes:** You are very aware of energy shifts in the environment through changes in taste.

23. **Taste Coincidences:** You experience frequent taste coincidences that guide your food choices.
24. **Flavor Confirmations:** You get taste-related confirmations, like tasting spices or ingredients that respond to your thoughts or questions.

These signs of Clairgustance can be both physical and deeply understanding. This sensory superpower and its signs will vary for each person in intensity and frequency. People who experience these signs often find them random and not controllable at first. Many choose to develop their abilities through meditation, psychic exercises, and learning from experts to harness and refine their talent.

Real Examples of Clairgustance

When I was only 15 years old, I encountered a phenomenon that only years later would I come to understand. Sitting at the back of a church, having had hotdogs with onions for dinner, I was conscious of my breath—which likely wasn't the freshest—and chose to sit away from the other youth at the front. Lost in thought and feeling grateful, I was suddenly struck by a taste so extraordinary it defies proper description. If I were to attempt it, I'd liken it to what is described as "nectar, sweeter than honey."

This taste blossomed subtly at first then rapidly filled my mouth, accompanied by an energizing sensation unlike anything I had previously known, or have known since—except on the rare occasions it recurs, which has been only four times in my life. Now familiar, yet still rare, this taste brings with it a rapturous, loving energy that envelops me completely, leaving me in awe of the profound state of love it induces. It served as a gateway to a new realization: our physical senses barely scratch the surface of a deeper reality that beckons, revealing glimpses of its richness sporadically throughout our lives.

Why don't we discuss these supernatural experiences more openly? Knowing that others share these experiences could reassure many that they are not alone, not anomalous.

Let me share about a profoundly intuitive massage therapist I met while living in Chattanooga, TN, at the Chattanooga Hotel Spa. After learning she made house calls, we began a professional relationship that deepened over time. I sensed she was intuitively reading my body during sessions, though initially, she was reticent to discuss it. Eventually, I encouraged her to share her insights openly, which marked the beginning of her embracing her Clairgustance. She could taste the energy blockages in a person's body while performing deep tissue massages, sometimes even before physically touching them. Her ability grew so refined she could anticipate the issues she would encounter in a client's body through taste.

Often, when clients came to my home for their private Life & Breakthrough Transformations, I would gift them a session with her as part of their healing journey. She cherished each person she worked with, and her skill became so acute that, by the time she arrived at my house, I would have fresh gum and cash ready for her. This was because I knew the emotional releases my clients would experience would also manifest physically, which she would then address with her unique skills.

Leaving Chattanooga—and her—was profoundly difficult; her Clairgustant abilities made her an unparalleled asset in physical and emotional healing. What a remarkable sense to explore!

My son-in-law Tanner has one of the most heightened senses of this ability of anyone I know other than my previous massage therapist. For years, as I visited my daughter and him and he created these delectable meals, I wouldn't take a bite, until he went through his presentation of what he had done, what we were eating, and the process he did to create it. I was shocked at how easily he detected the nuance of over-mixing something in a blender and how he could pick that up and distinguish the difference between a second or two in cooking something to culinary perfection.

This ability has served him well as an Executive Chef and he speaks of the ingredients of a new dish easily for he knows the taste and essence of them so much that the smallest of changes in the preparation, makes the entire dish something different. My daughter and I have fun together discussing food a lot, for we are all foodies. Their three children are learning this discerning sensory superpower.

Benefits of Tasting in Communication

In Relationships:

Clairgustance can boost how well you understand others, going beyond just talking. This ability lets you taste the emotional "flavor" of someone's feelings, giving you a unique edge in all kinds of relationships.

If you have this superpower, you naturally understand emotions and can sense what people feel in the moment, and the energy behind their words. This helps you respond with kindness and understanding, making your connections with others stronger and more meaningful.

By tasting possible misunderstandings or the emotional "flavors" of conflicts, a Clairgustant can address problems before they get worse, helping to keep peace in relationships.

Tasting things from someone else's point of view can build empathy and understanding, making relationships more supportive and caring.

In Monetizing:

In the business world, this sensory superpower can be a game-changer. This ability helps you make smart decisions by understanding the "flavors" of conversations, team dynamics, and competition that others might miss.

Clairgustants can offer their unique insights to people or businesses, guiding them on personal choices or business strategies. You become a valuable consultant because of your special talent to taste and interpret the unspoken.

With this skill, you can handle negotiations with a sense of foresight, leading to better outcomes and potential financial gains.

Getting Clarity on Others:

Your Clairgustance abilities are useful as a valuable tool to discern the true intentions and honesty of others and can safeguard you from being manipulated. This innate superpower builds your intuition and discernment, allowing you to gauge whether you can trust people in both personal and professional relationships.

By knowing what someone needs and likes, you can communicate in a way that they appreciate and understand. This deeper connection makes people want to be around you and as with the other superpowers, do business with you.

Cultivating Clairgustance for Growth:

Practicing mindfulness and taste-focused exercises regularly can make your clear-tasting stronger and more accurate.

Sharing your insights with others and getting feedback can help you understand your Clairgustant experiences better.

Reading books and taking courses on this superpower and psychic and spiritual development can give you the tools and techniques to use this ability more effectively for your success in all things in life.

Expanding Clairgustant Abilities:

Regularly practice exercises that improve your ability to taste skills and help you recognize and define the flavors you sense.

Learn and practice meditations that focus on different flavors or food smells to become more aware of them.

Join groups or communities focused on psychic development to get support and share experiences, which can help you grow this Clair-sense faster.

By doing these practices, Clairgustance can improve not only your ability to clear-taste but also your relationships and open up new chances for professional growth and financial success.

Potential Challenges of Clairgustance if Mismanaged or Unrecognized

Having this sensory superpower can bring unique challenges. Here are some issues that people with this ability might face:

1. **Overload:** Getting constant or strong clear-tasting information can be overwhelming, leading to sensory overload or mental exhaustion.
2. **Confusion:** It can be hard to tell the difference between real tastes and the ones perceived through this ability, which can be disorienting.
3. **Negative Flavors:** Tasting flavors linked to bad experiences or emotions can cause anxiety or fear.
4. **Privacy Issues:** They might taste sensitive information about others, leading to ethical dilemmas and privacy concerns.
5. **Misinterpretation:** There's a risk of misunderstanding these sensory insights, which can lead to wrong decisions or spreading false information.
6. **Skepticism:** Facing disbelief from others can make people with these abilities feel isolated or doubt themselves.
7. **Social Stigma:** Psychic abilities might carry a social stigma, affecting personal and professional relationships.

8. **Mental Health Concerns:** Clairgustants may worry about their mental health, fearing they might be seen as delusional or unstable.
9. **Physical Symptoms:** Some people report feeling nauseous or having changes in appetite because of their ability to read energy in taste.
10. **Relationship Strain:** Friends and family might not understand or accept their real experiences, straining relationships.
11. **Boundary Issues:** Clairgustants might struggle to separate their tastes from those they perceive from others, leading to emotional entanglement.
12. **Responsibility:** Handling the information gained through clear-tasting comes with ethical considerations about when and how to share it.
13. **Distraction:** Focusing too much on Clairgustant perceptions can distract from living in the present and handling everyday tasks.
14. **Unrealistic Expectations:** People might expect too much from this sensory ability, assuming their abilities are flawless and can solve all problems, causing stress.
15. **Personal Use:** People with this ability can often help others with their ability but might not use it for their benefit.

Learning how to manage this sensory superpower and finding a balance can help mitigate these challenges. Setting healthy boundaries, developing coping strategies, and seeking support from understanding communities are important. Guidance from experienced Clairgustants can help them navigate their abilities and use them successfully.

Career Paths for Clairgustance

Culinary Arts Expert: They have a special ability to detect and work with subtle flavors, making them great chefs, food critics, or culinary consultants. They can start new culinary trends or improve traditional recipes by balancing ingredients in creative ways. Their amazing sense of taste is also important in creating new food and drink products in the hospitality industry.

Food and Beverage Product Development: In food science and product development, people with these abilities can help create new products or make existing ones better by understanding what consumers like and predicting flavor trends. Their sharp sense of taste helps fine-tune flavors before products hit the market, ensuring they meet consumer expectations and stand out.

Sommelier or Beverage Tasting Consultant: Clairgustants can excel as sommeliers or beverage tasters, using their refined palate to understand and explain the details of wine, coffee, craft beers, and other drinks. They can help restaurants, bars, and private clients choose the best beverages to enhance dining experiences.

Quality Control Specialist: In manufacturing and production, people with this sensory superpower are perfect for quality control jobs, especially in the food and beverage sectors. Their ability to detect even the slightest change in taste ensures consistent product quality and safety.

Nutritional Therapist: They can offer unique insights as nutritional therapists, using their ability to taste and sense the energy in foods. They can create diet plans that focus on both nutrition and how foods feel energetically, helping clients improve their physical and emotional well-being.

Aromatherapy and Herbal Medicine: This sensory superpower often has a strong sense of smell too, making them great for careers in aromatherapy and herbal medicine. They can create powerful blends of essential oils or herbal remedies that are both effective and pleasant.

Wellness Coach or Spiritual Advisor: Clairgustants who understand the emotional and spiritual meanings of tastes can work as wellness coaches or spiritual advisors. They can use their abilities to help clients find balance and harmony, guiding them through sensory experiences that promote healing and personal growth.

Research and Development: In academic or industrial research, they can contribute to studies on taste perception, food preferences, and dietary solutions. Their enhanced sense of taste allows them to participate in groundbreaking research that can influence public health policies or commercial food production strategies.

Educator and Trainer: They can teach others about the complexities of taste and flavor as culinary school instructors or corporate trainers for food and beverage companies. They can create training programs to improve the gustatory skills of aspiring chefs, bartenders, or food enthusiasts.

Entrepreneur: Clairgustants can start their businesses in the food and beverage industry, creating unique dining experiences, launching innovative food products, or offering consultancy services that use their extraordinary sensory skills.

By using their special sensory abilities in their careers, people with this sensory superpower can explore various paths that allow them to share their unique perceptions, improving both their own lives and the lives of others around them.

Detecting Clairgustance in Others

Recognizing clear-tasting abilities in others allows for deeper interaction and understanding. Here's how you might detect Clairgustance:

Observational Signs:

They might respond to questions or comments that relate to taste or food without them being explicitly mentioned, indicating they've sensed flavors or tastes that have not been spoken about.

Listen to whether they appear to be reacting to flavors or tastes that aren't physically present, as if savoring something that others cannot perceive.

Notice if they often seem to react to flavors or food-related sensations that are not apparent to others, as if catching a subtle taste carried by the air.

Behavioral Indicators:

They may speak of tasting things before they occur, such as predicting the flavor of a meal before it is served or reacting to a food's taste before trying it.

A strong reaction to the flavor or essence in someone's cooking, even when the ingredients are ordinary, can indicate Clairgustant sensitivity.

They might discuss tasting distinct flavors or foods in their dreams that later manifest in reality, or share culinary insights gained from dream experiences.

Communicating with a Clairgustant Individual:

Be clear and straightforward in your discussions about food and flavors. Clairgustants may pick up on the subtle undertones of your culinary preferences or the hidden flavors behind your meals or what you are speaking about, for this ability goes beyond the natural taste. They have a heightened sense of awareness about how something is going to go or present itself in life.

Engage in discussions about metaphysical things which can include taste-related topics.

Validate their experiences without judgment, which can encourage open and honest communication about their taste insights.

Helping Others Understand Clairgustant Messages:

Instead of saying, "I taste something unusual," try saying, "I sense a unique flavor or essence that might mean..."

Talk about times when Clairgustance has given you useful information. Share stories where your ability to taste has led to important insights or discoveries, making it easier for others to understand.

Help others notice subtle sensory cues that might relate to Clairgustance. Encourage them to pay attention to faint tastes or sensations that could carry deeper messages. Ask them to go deeper into something they are speaking of.

Present your tasting insights in ways that relate to everyday issues or decisions. Show how gustatory perceptions can lead to practical outcomes or solutions, demonstrating their usefulness in daily life.

Cultivating a Supportive Environment for Clairgustants:

Provide thorough explanations about what clear-tasting is and help them with any misconceptions. Educating others helps demystify this less commonly understood sensory ability.

It is crucial to respect personal boundaries when sharing or discussing these sensory superpower experiences. Prioritize obtaining consent and maintaining comfort levels to ensure respectful and ethical interactions.

Encourage skepticism and critical questions among peers and colleagues. This approach helps validate your superpower experiences and fosters a balanced understanding of these sensory messages.

Collaborative Engagement with Clairgustant

Use clear-tasting as a new tool in team brainstorming and planning sessions. The unique taste-based insights from you can lead to better ideas and strategies.

This sensory superpower can add a new dimension to creative work like cooking, product development, and marketing. Their deep understanding of flavors can inspire fresh ideas and innovations.

As with all of the sensory superpowers, use your heightened tasting abilities ethically, respecting people's privacy and emotional well-being.

When you communicate with Clairgustants consider that they need sensitivity and openness. By creating an environment of respect and understanding, These skills can enhance both personal relationships and professional teamwork. This approach improves team dynamics and drives innovation, especially in food, beverage, and flavor-related fields.

Clear-tasting can help solve complex problems in these areas by providing deep insights into consumer preferences and product potential based on subtle taste differences.

By understanding these signs, you can better interact with clear-tasters, building relationships that benefit from mutual understanding and respect.

Practical Exercises for Clairgustants

Developing this sensory superpower involves improving your ability to discern and understand subtle tastes that are not physically present. Here are some practical exercises to refine your Clairgustant abilities:

Sensory Recall Practice: Select different foods you know well and taste them one by one. After tasting each item, step away from any food, then try to recall and mentally re-experience the taste. This exercise helps you remember specific flavors without actually eating them and connects you to your abilities in a deeper way.

Concentrated Flavor Meditation: Choose a flavor to focus on, such as lemon, chocolate, or salt. Close your eyes, clear your mind, and try to feel this flavor in your mouth without eating it. This meditation improves your focus and ability to create detailed taste perceptions in your mind.

Blind Taste Testing: With a friend's help, try blind taste tests using small amounts of various foods and spices. Identify the substances based solely on their taste without seeing them. This sharpens your taste buds and helps you notice subtle differences in flavors.

Aroma-to-Taste Transformation: Smell various herbs, spices, or other aromatic substances and try to imagine how they would taste in your mouth. This practice helps bridge the connection between your sense of smell and your sense of taste, improving them both.

Journaling Flavor Profiles: Keep a journal of the tastes you experience throughout the day, both physical and those perceived through your tasting superpower. Note any emotional or physical sensations associated with these tastes. Journaling helps in documenting and making sense of the Clairgustant experiences, aiding in recognizing patterns or triggers.

Progressive Relaxation for Enhanced Sensitivity: Practice relaxing your muscles techniques, especially in your mouth, throat, and nose. Relaxing these specific areas can heighten sensitivity to taste and smells, making your tasting superpower much clearer and distinguishable for you.

Flavor Pairing Visualization: Imagine how different foods combine before preparing or tasting them. Visualize how different ingredients change the outcome of a dish you are thinking of preparing. This exercise enhances your creativity in combining tastes and improves your predictive tasting superpowers.

Ethical Practice Reflections: Reflect regularly on the ethical implications of your heightened sense of taste, especially regarding privacy and personal boundaries. This helps you use your abilities with integrity for others.

These exercises not only improve your Clairgustant abilities but also help you appreciate and integrate your unique sensory experiences into your daily life and personal growth.

Progressive Training for Clairgustance

Each exercise in this chapter builds upon the previous, starting from simple taste-focused exercises to more complex guided tastings that encourage deeper sensory development. By practicing these exercises regularly, you'll enhance not only your tasting superpowers but also your overall sensory awareness. The goal is not just to taste beyond the physical but to connect with and understand the deeper layers of information that Clairgustance can reveal. This progressive training will prepare you for more advanced tasting work, like flavor analysis and other sensory practices.

By dedicating time to these exercises and meditations, you lay a strong foundation for your clear-tasting journey, paving the way for profound insights and improved intuitive taste capabilities. As you progress, remember that patience and consistency are key in unlocking the full potential of your gustatory senses.

Understanding and recognizing tasting superpowers in oneself and others can significantly enhance your appreciation of human sensory experiences.

Clairgustants have the unique ability to perceive and interpret the world through flavors, offering insights that transcend regular sensory boundaries. This heightened sensitivity to taste can deepen personal relationships, create unique career opportunities, and give you a richer perspective on life.

By fostering an environment of openness and acceptance around embracing the symphony of taste, you are encouraged to explore and develop your abilities fully. As you continue to embrace and understand this extraordinary sensory capacity, you can unlock a world of potential that can enrich both our culinary and interpersonal experiences. This tasting sensory ability is not just about tasting food; it's about tasting life itself, in all its varied and flavorful dimensions.

If you're eager to enhance your Clairgustance abilities and unlock your full potential, consider enrolling in a specialized course designed specifically for mastering these skills. Sign up for the "Awakening Your Superpowers" class https://superpowersunleashed.com. This course is carefully crafted to navigate the subtleties of this superpower, empowering you to harness these abilities for personal advancement and professional success. Take action today to activate your sensory superpowers and transform how you tackle life's challenges and opportunities.

To further your exploration of mastering your tasting superpower and to connect with others who share your interests globally, refer to the Free Resources page to find out how you can be supported further.

In the next chapter, we will delve into Clairscent. Let's go!

CHAPTER 5:
WHISPERS OF THE INVISIBLE
Mastering The Essence of Clairscent

Welcome to the amazing world of Clairscent, where you unlock the secrets of the seen and unseen aromas. This ability lets you detect and understand special fragrances carried by the winds of the universe. In this chapter, we'll explore the mysterious nature of clear-smelling and how it can heighten your awareness of the present, but will also connect you to mystical messages.

Clairscent, or "clear smelling," is the sense that lets you perceive smells beyond what most people smell. This could include sensing the fragrance of spiritual presences, emotional imprints in places, or even the unique scents of different dimensions. Unlike ordinary smelling, this sensory superpower often involves detecting aromas that bring guidance, warnings, or insights.

The journey to recognizing Clairscent begins with noticing its subtle signs. You might smell fragrances where there are none present, or notice scents connected to certain emotions or memories. These experiences are not just figments of your imagination, they are profound messages meant just for you. Early signs might also include a heightened sensitivity to certain smells, serving to help you tune into this sense.

In practical terms, clear-smelling can be very helpful. It offers deeper empathy and understanding in personal and professional interactions. For example, by sensing the underlying emotional atmosphere of a room, you can better navigate social situations more effectively to make more informed decisions during negotiations.

To develop Clairscent you'll need attention, meditation, and practice. Start by consciously noticing the smells around you, both obvious and subtle. Meditation can help quiet the mind, making it easier to discern and understand the spiritual or emotional nuances that everyday life reveals. Practicing mindful awareness of your surroundings can further refine your smelling abilities, helping you discern not just the physical scents but also the messages they convey about the unseen world.

As your smelling superpowers grow stronger, you may find yourself forging deeper connections with the spiritual realms or engaging more profoundly with people through the universal language of scent. This connection can offer comfort, guidance, and validation of a reality beyond our physical senses.

Clairscent provides invaluable insights when making decisions, helping you to make the right choices by catching the subtle scents of opportunity or caution. This guidance is especially useful in moments of uncertainty or when at an important crossroads in life.

By opening yourself to a deeper understanding of the universe through the often-overlooked sense of smell, this superpower equips you with wisdom that goes beyond the physical world of scents. This chapter invites you to explore this divine spectrum of scents, enriching your life with wisdom beyond the tangible world.

This chapter aims to comprehensively explore Clairscent, from recognizing its signs to using its insights in daily life. By embracing the symphony of the invisible, you can experience life with a perspective deeply rooted in both the seen and unseen realms.

The concept of Clairscent, or "clear smelling," is a lesser-known but fascinating aspect of extrasensory perception (ESP). This sensory ability allows you to perceive scents and odors beyond the physical world, often linked with spiritual or metaphysical experiences.

Here is an Overview of the History of Clairgustance

The idea of smelling and perceiving scents that aren't physically present has been around in many ancient cultures. In ancient Egypt, incense was believed to carry prayers to the gods, and being able to smell divine fragrances was considered a sign of favor or a message from the divine. Similarly, in Hinduism, using aromatic incense in rituals is thought to please the gods and facilitate spiritual experiences, showing an early belief in the power of scent beyond the physical world.

During the Middle Ages and the Renaissance, mystical or supernatural scents were often connected with religious experiences. Mystics and saints reported smelling heavenly fragrances—such as flowers or incense that weren't there, as a sign of a divine presence or spiritual revelation. One famous example is St. Teresa of Avila, who reported smelling divine scents during her mystical encounters.

The 19th century saw a surge in interest in spiritualism and the occult in Europe and America. During séances, during sessions, and spiritual gatherings, mediums often claimed to smell flowers or other scents as a sign that spirits were present. This era popularized the idea that scents bridge the living with the spiritual world in a direct and personal way.

In the 20th century, parapsychologists began to study psychic phenomena, including Clairscent, under more scientific conditions. Researchers like J.B. Rhine at Duke University explored ESP and related phenomena, trying to establish evidence for these experiences. While this sense was less studied than other psychic abilities, such as Clairvoyance or telepathy, it remained a topic of interest for those studying the non-physical senses and their impact on the human experience.

Today, clear-smelling is recognized by people having heightened psychic sensitivities. It is often discussed in holistic and spiritual practices as a tool for deeper spiritual connection and insight. Practitioners of modern spirituality might use clear-smelling to detect the presence of spiritual entities, to receive guidance or warnings, or to enhance their other psychic abilities.

The study of this sensory superpower, though not as popular as other psychic phenomena, continues to fascinate those interested in the limits of human perception and the connection between the physical and spiritual realms. As with many of the paranormal studies, it challenges our understanding of reality and raises questions about what is truly possible in human experience.

Famous Historical Figure with Clairscent

One notable historical figure reputed to have experienced Clairscent is Saint Padre Pio, a 20th-century Italian priest who was made a saint by the Catholic Church. Padre Pio is famous for his stigmata, (wounds similar to those of Jesus), mystical experiences, and miraculous healings. Among his many spiritual gifts was also the uncanny ability to sense smells not physically present.

Saint Padre Pio reportedly could extraordinarily smell the spiritual state of people who came to him for his counsel. He could detect the scent of sanctity, which was like floral fragrances, indicating a pure soul or divine presence. On the other hand, he could smell the odor of sin or evil, such as sulfur or smoke, which warned him of the spiritual dangers or the moral state of individuals. This ability played a significant role helping him guide and counsel people who came to him.

Padre Pio often used his sense of smell to diagnose the spiritual condition of the people who came to him for confession or counseling. This ability reportedly helped him provide tailored spiritual guidance and offer penance for the specific needs of each person.

He also reported smelling the odor of demons during exorcisms or when confronting evil, which he described as the stench of burning sulfur.

Padre Pio's experiences with Clairscent are extensively documented in many biographies and accounts by those who knew him. These stories and illustrations highlight the significance as part of his spiritual and religious life. His life and abilities continue to fascinate and inspire many within the Catholic community and beyond, showing how this superpower, like other psychic phenomena, can deeply connect with personal spirituality and religious service.

Where is it located?

Clairscent, the ability to detect ethereal aromas and messages, going beyond ordinary smelling and includes deeper spiritual awareness. This unique sensory superpower is not centered in the nose but is linked to the area around the heart chakra, located at the center of the chest. This specific region energetically connects to emotional insight and relationships and serves as a bridge between physical smelling and profound spiritual revelations.

Fragrance experts, such as perfumers known for their intuitive blending, often describe the precise location of this sense. They often place their hand on their chest before blending a new fragrance, unknowingly engaging their Clairscent ability. This habit highlights the deep connection between the physical and spiritual aspects of scent, even in professional settings where creating precise and emotionally resonant scents is crucial.

Through this energetic center near the heart, people with clear smells perceive subtle fragrances and turn them into meaningful insights. They can detect scents that go beyond normal smelling. In this special area where the physical and the spiritual meet, Clairscent offers not only a way to smell but also the messages carried by scents, both detected and felt. This integration helps those with this sensory superpower navigate both the visible and invisible realms, deciphering messages that go beyond ordinary perception.

Common Beginnings of Clairscent

1. **Unprompted Scents:** As mentioned, many people with Clairscent abilities report sensing scents without a physical source. This can happen in both waking states or dreams, including smelling specific aromas that are not physically there or scents linked to memories or emotional states.

2. **Subtle Smell Encounters**: They might detect faint smells that seem to hover at the edge of their awareness. These brief whiffs can disappear when directly focused upon. These can be puzzling, leading you to question if they are real. They are real and are in fact, genuine signs of these superpowers.

3. **Early Life Experiences:** Similar to Clairvoyants, those with Clairscent superpowers often become aware of their abilities early in life, frequently dismissing them as mere imagination. Kids might sense smells that adults can't or have a detailed awareness of smells related to memories they haven't directly experienced, often thought to be messages from unseen entities.

4. **Increased Sensitivity:** Those with this superpower typically have a heightened sensitivity to aromas. They notice minor changes in scents or the emotional nuances associated with specific environments,

allowing them to "smell" what is and isn't visibly present.

5. **Life-Altering Events:** Clairscent abilities may also appear following significant life changes or traumatic events such as near-death experiences, severe illnesses, or major emotional losses, which can start a shift in sensory perception, enhancing the olfactory senses to perceive beyond the typical.

6. **Natural Echoes:** Some individuals discover that their clear-smelling abilities are triggered or intensified by the natural elements they are exposed to. The scent of plants, the smell of rain, or the distinct aromas of changing seasons might initiate or deepen the clear-smelling abilities. This creates a strong connection to the natural world.

7. **Environmental Stimuli:** Interestingly, certain environmental exposures, like the aroma of modern materials or chemical scents, can provoke heightened smelling episodes. This might include detecting unusual scents in urban settings or when interacting with new synthetic materials. Could be fabric or otherwise.

8. **Meditative and Spiritual Practices:** Regular meditation, prayer, or spiritual practices can greatly

enhance Clairscent abilities. These practices quiet the mind and make it more receptive to subtle olfactory signals, often hidden in daily life. Deep meditation is especially effective in opening the olfactory channels to spiritual insights.

9. **Cultural and Ritual Practices:** In various cultures, ritual practices involving specific herbs, spices, or ceremonial incense can awaken or amplify clear-smelling abilities. These rituals often establish a pathway to trance states, making clear-smelling perceptions more accessible.

10. **Enhanced Perception in Social Contexts:** People with superpower smelling abilities perceive and interpret scents in social settings, such as gatherings or events, in ways others can't. This heightened awareness enables them to sense underlying messages or emotional residues in the atmosphere, providing significant insights into social dynamics and aiding in both personal and professional interactions.

11. **Sudden Clarity in Fragrant Settings:** Some first become aware of their Clairscent abilities when they clearly smell and understand aromas in environments that overwhelm others with a mixture of scents. They may identify specific elements in a complex scent or

discern subtle fragrances that others miss. This skill often emerges unexpectedly, revealing layers of olfactory information that offer insights into the surroundings or the emotions and intentions of people nearby.

Understanding these common beginnings helps you better recognize and cultivate your smelling superpowers, integrating them into your everyday life or spiritual practices for deeper personal insight and growth.

Signs of Emerging Clairscent

Clairscent is a type of extrasensory perception (ESP), that enables people to discern scents. This ability connects to a deeper spiritual or energetic level bridging the gap between the physical and metaphysical realms.

1. **How it works:** The physical sense involves the olfactory system, which includes the nose and the olfactory receptors. Normally, scent molecules send signals to the brain to recognize specific odors. However, in Clairscent, these scents are perceived as absent without any direct physical sources. It's as if the brain receives these scent signals directly from a non-physical source.

2. **Nervous System Integration:** Those experiencing clear-smelling superpowers might feel like recalling a scent or experiencing a strong scent association triggered by a memory or an emotion that has not been healed within. The key difference is that this superpower can happen spontaneously and isn't necessarily linked to recent smells or physical triggers. This suggests that this superpower uses unique neural pathways that bypass typical sensory methods, directly engaging parts of the brain responsible for scent awareness.

3. **Psychic and Spiritual Connection:** This sensory superpower is intricately tied to physical and nonphysical realms. It is believed to facilitate people receiving messages or insights from spiritual guides, deceased loved ones, or the collective unconscious. These messages often come through symbolic scents. For example, smelling roses might indicate a loving presence or good news, while a scent of smoke might signal a warning or a negative presence.

4. **Emotional and Energetic Resonance:** Scents can evoke powerful emotional responses and are intimately tied to memory and feelings. In Clairscent, the odors experienced may correspond to specific emotional or

energetic states of others or of a specific location. For instance, you might smell freshness and earthiness around someone feeling joy or renewal, or detect a musty odor in a place with a somber history.

5. **Practical Applications:** This superpower can be valuable in various fields, including perfumery, therapy, and spiritual healing. Perfumers might innovate new fragrances, while therapists might use them to gain insights into their clients' emotional states. In spiritual practices, it can be used for purification rituals or to discern the presence of specific energies or entities.

6. **Development and Refinement:** Like other psychic abilities, clear-smelling can be honed through practice and meditation. Techniques might include focusing on the sensation of smelling while meditating, clearing the mind to receive information on subtle energies, or focusing on a lit candle and seeing what comes forward in smell.

Understanding this sensory superpower involves acknowledging its profound connection to both the physical senses and deeper metaphysical insights. It transcends ordinary sensory experiences, offering a unique and often enlightening perspective on the world.

Clairscent is fascinating and is a complex sensory ability that bridges the gap between the physical and spiritual realms, allowing for unique communication through the sense of smell. By transcending the ordinary sensory smelling experiences, it provides a great tool for insight and connection, revealing hidden emotional landscapes and spiritual messages. Those who develop this ability gain a deeper understanding of the world, enhance their relationships, and gain a richer, more nuanced perspective on life. As we continue to explore and understand this superpower, it deepens our connection to both the seen and unseen aspects of our lives.

Signs You Have Clairscent

Clairscent involves a heightened intuitive ability to perceive smells beyond what the ordinary senses typically detect. Here are some indications of clear-smelling:

1. **Olfactory Hallucinations:** Smelling scents, aromas, or fragrances that are not physically present.
2. **Precognitive Smelling:** Smelling scents that foretell future events.
3. **Telepathic Smelling:** Smelling what someone else is experiencing, even from far away, as if you are directly smelling it.

4. **Smelling Auras:** Detecting scents or essences around people, animals, or objects that others cannot smell.
5. **Spiritual Scents:** Smelling aromas associated with spiritual entities, guides, or angelic beings that aren't visible.
6. **Symbolic Scents:** Experiencing scents in dreams that carry messages or predict future events.
7. **Peripheral Scents:** Detecting faint scents that seem to come from nowhere, often just outside clear focus.
8. **Heart Chakra Activity:** Feeling sensations in or around the chest area, like warmth or tingling, related to the energy centers associated with Clairscent.
9. **Sudden Clarity:** Receiving clear olfactory insights or solutions to problems without a logical reason for them coming to you.
10. **Recognizing Patterns:** Noticing olfactory patterns or sequences that seem to convey important messages or warnings.
11. **Deja Smell:** Experiencing strong sensations of familiarity with a specific scent or aroma.
12. **Vivid Smelling in Dreams:** Having dreams with distinct olfactory experiences that feel as real as life and may provide information about future events.

13. **Psychic Scents:** Experiencing lingering smells that give insight or understanding about situations or people.
14. **Intuitive Smelling:** Developing a keen sense of underlying truths in environments or encounters, beyond what is physically present.
15. **Vivid Scent-scapes**: Encountering exceptionally clear and memorable olfactory experiences in dreams that carry significant messages.
16. **Energetic Chest Sensations:** Feeling activity, like fluttering or pulsing, in the chest area, often linked to the energetic perception of scent.
17. **Natural Affinity:** Having a strong, innate interest in olfactory practices, like perfumery or aromatherapy, even if not pursued before.
18. **Spontaneous Understanding:** Suddenly understanding complex scents or the emotional states of others through subtle changes in scent.
19. **Accurate Predictions:** Experiencing olfactory premonitions about events or emotional shifts that prove to be accurate.
20. **Symbolic Language:** Understanding the symbolic meanings of scents or aromas that appear in your mind or dreams.

21. **Receiving Guidance:** Feeling as though specific olfactory advice or warnings are communicated directly to you, especially regarding future health or current conditions.

22. **Sensitivity to Scent-Scapes:** Having a heightened awareness of energy shifts in the environment, perceived through changes in scents or the sudden emergence of smells.

23. **Olfactory Synchronicities:** Experiencing frequent coincidental scents that seem to guide or inform your decisions about your environment or well-being.

24. **Affirmations from Scents:** Receiving confirmations from the olfactory environment, like smelling relevant fragrances or scents that respond to your thoughts or questions.

These signs of Clairscent can create a profound sense of understanding and communication. It's important to note that this superpower and its signs are deeply personal and can vary in intensity and frequency. Individuals who experience these signs often describe them as sporadic and not within their control, at least initially. Many choose to further develop these abilities through practices like meditation, mindfulness, and other spiritual exercises.

Real Examples of Clairscent

From a young age, I faced a unique challenge with my sense of smell. At eleven, I mysteriously lost it. The surgeon I went to in my twenties said it was due to an abnormal tooth that developed in my nasal cavity. My ability to smell was sporadic; occasionally, I'd catch the faint scent of a rose by pressing my nose deeply into it, but more often than not, I detected nothing.

This off-and-on ability to smell led to some unusual social situations. On the rare occasions when I could smell someone during a hug, I would excitedly ask them to pause, hoping to savor the fleeting aroma a bit longer, though often the scent would vanish as quickly as it came.

Perfume became a source of anxiety for me. Without a reliable sense of smell, I was constantly worried about over-applying it. Family car rides often began with windows rolled down to help them deal with how much perfume I had put on. I couldn't smell how much I sprayed and would try to wipe it off as much as I could before we arrived at our destination. We laughed about it, but it was awkward for me.

In stores, when someone would say, "You smell so good"! I would anxiously ask strangers if I could ask them this question, "If you don't mind me asking, how far away from me did you smell my perfume? Sometimes I don't know how much I'm putting on", The people were always kind and smiled at me and told me not that far away. After years of this, I finally stopped wearing perfume altogether. I still get told that I smell good now, but have no idea what they smell but am thankful that it is pleasing to some.

Despite these challenges with the physical sense of smell, I've had profound experiences with scent in my professional intuitive work. During sessions with clients, I sometimes perceive specific scents—like a cigar, a violet, or an unfamiliar food and when they come, I get the intuitive information of what they are, for I cannot identify them personally. These scents aren't just random; they hold significant meaning for the client, providing personal reassurance and a sense of being deeply understood and cared for.

Interestingly, I once dated a man with the extraordinarily developed sense of smell of anyone I'd ever met. He could detect the mood and thoughts of others just by their scent. His ability to read emotions through olfactory cues was fascinating. He often described my emotional and mental state just by smelling the air around me, providing shockingly accurate insights. This relationship deepened my understanding of Clairscent, revealing the extent a scent can convey the essence of a person's soul.

After we parted ways and later reconnected, he confessed that what he missed most was the unique sweetness and purity he could smell around me—qualities he said were due to the personal healing work I had accomplished in life. His awareness of the inner work that he could smell, was a profound thing to learn about clear-smelling. He wasn't a spiritual person, but had an inherent knowing because he said he'd never smelled anyone like this before.

He also read my family members but hesitated to let me know what he was picking up on them, especially one specifically. I knew it was because he was sensing something sensual in nature emanating from her, even though it may or may not have been directed at him solely.

Watching him and hearing his remarks while we dated for a short time, made me realize the unlimited potential of our senses. This scent superpower, particularly in someone so attuned, can access understanding far beyond the physical, tapping into the very essence of our being. This experience taught me just how integral our non-physical attributes are to our interactions and relationships, offering a window into the soul that transcends conventional sensory experiences.

Benefits of Smelling in Communication

In Relationships:

Clairscent can greatly improve communication in relationships by enabling a deeper understanding of others beyond just words. The ability to smell the emotional essence or the 'scent' of someone's state of mind or feelings provides a unique advantage across all relationships.

People with clear-smelling have a natural ability to detect emotions, allowing them to sense the feelings and intentions behind what others say. This olfactory emotional intelligence can deepen bonds and create more meaningful connections.

By sensing potential misunderstandings or the emotional scents of conflicts, a Clairscent person can address issues before they escalate, fostering harmony in relationships.

Smelling things from the perspective of another enhances empathy and understanding, leading to more supportive and nurturing relationships.

It can also give cues as to desires that are normal to experience and want as humans and being able to pick up on that scent is a wonderful tool to use to help meet the needs of others personally.

In Monetizing:

In the business world, this superpower can be monetized through strategic decisions based on insights into conversational scents, team, and competitive dynamics that others might miss.

Individuals with Clairscent can offer their services to guide others on personal life decisions or business strategies, becoming valuable consultants due to their ability to interpret and understand scents.

With the capacity to smell the unspoken, they can navigate negotiations with foresight, leading to better outcomes and potential financial gains.

Getting Clarity on Others:

Discerning the true intentions and integrity of others through their scent can protect against deception, ensuring trust in both personal and professional relationships.

Understanding specific emotional needs and preferences allows for tailored communication that is more effective and appreciated, enhancing interpersonal connections.

Cultivating Clairscent for Growth:

Engaging regularly in mindfulness and exercises focused on smelling can sharpen this sensory-smelling superpower. This will help you have clearer intuition and be able to interpret interactions that enable you to have an advantage in life.

Sharing insights and receiving feedback can help you better understand and interpret your Clairscent experiences.

Exploring books and courses on clear-smelling and psychic development can provide essential tools and techniques to effectively harness this ability.

Expanding Clairscent Abilities:

Engage regularly in exercises designed to improve your smelling skills and your ability to interpret olfactory information.

Practicing meditations focused on different scents or aromatic essences can increase sensitivity to olfactory cues.

Joining and participating in groups or communities centered on sensory and spiritual development can offer support and shared experiences, accelerating personal growth.

Incorporating these practices not only improves and enriches personal relationships but also opens opportunities for professional advancement and financial opportunities.

Potential Challenges of Clairscent if Mismanaged or Unrecognized

Having Clairscent abilities can bring unique challenges. Here are some potential issues that people with clear-smelling might face:

1. **Sensory Overload:** Constant or intense superpowered smells can be overwhelming, leading to sensory overload or mental exhaustion. This might make it hard to filter out background smells, causing distraction or irritation.
2. **Confusion:** It can be challenging to tell the difference between scents from the spiritual or nonphysical realm and those in the physical world, which can be confusing or disorienting.
3. **Emotional Impact:** Smelling odors associated with negative experiences or emotions can have a strong emotional impact, leading to anxiety or fear.
4. **Privacy Concerns:** Clairscent individuals might unintentionally pick up private scents or impressions not meant to be perceived, leading to discomfort or ethical dilemmas.
5. **Misinterpretation:** There is always a risk of misinterpreting these superpower messages, which can result in making incorrect decisions or spreading misinformation.
6. **Skepticism and Isolation:** Encountering skepticism or disbelief from others can lead to feelings of isolation or self-doubt.

7. **Social Signs:** Psychic abilities might carry a social stigma, affecting personal and professional relationships and leading to social isolation.
8. **Mental Health Concerns:** Clairscent people, just like all the other sensory superpowers, might question their mental health, especially when they begin to experience these phenomena, due to fear of being labeled as delusional or mentally unstable.
9. **Physical Symptoms:** Some people report physical symptoms, like headaches or nausea, particularly when their abilities become active.
10. **Relationship Strain:** Friends and family might have trouble understanding or accepting the smelling superpower experiences, which can strain relationships.
11. **Emotional Boundaries:** It can be difficult to maintain emotional boundaries between their feelings and the emotions they perceive from others, leading to emotional entanglement or a sense of intrusion.
12. **Responsibility and Ethics:** Handling the information gained through these abilities comes with significant responsibility, including ethical considerations about when and how to share it.

13. **Distraction From the Present:** A strong focus on olfactory messages can sometimes distract from living in the present moment and attending to immediate, practical aspects of life.
14. **Unrealistic Expectations:** Others might have unrealistic expectations of these abilities, assuming they are infallible or that the Clairscent individual can solve all problems, leading to pressure and stress.
15. **Social Withdrawal:** Sometimes, Clairscent individuals might want to avoid social gatherings and crowded places to manage overwhelming olfactory input and find peace.
16. **Assimilating Scents:** They might struggle with perceiving too many scents at once and not knowing how to process that information. Ambient smells can be particularly challenging because they may not know how to single out the scents they want to focus on.

People with clear-scent abilities often benefit from learning how to manage their superpower and find a balance to deal with these potential issues. This can involve setting healthy boundaries, developing coping strategies, and seeking support from understanding communities. Getting guidance from a highly developed Clairscent person can be especially helpful in learning to navigate their abilities and use them successfully.

Career Paths for Clairscents

Developing Clairscent abilities can lead to unique and fulfilling careers, especially in fields that benefit from a heightened sense of smell and a deep understanding of emotions and environments. Here are some potential career paths for those with these abilities:

Perfumery and Fragrance Designing: Use your clear-smelling abilities to create unique and complex fragrances. Work in perfume manufacturing, and scent branding for companies, or start your own boutique fragrance business.

Aromatherapy: Use essential oils and aromatic compounds for healing and wellness. Offer services in spas, wellness centers, or private practice, focusing on holistic health solutions.

Wine and Food Industry: As a wine sommelier, use your super sense of smell to detect subtle nuances in wine, enhancing tasting experiences for clients. As a food critic or flavor consultant, provide expert opinions and advice based on your enhanced olfactory abilities. Or as a chef where you can constantly explore the flavors of life through food.

Environmental Science: Use your smelling superpower to detect pollutants or toxins in the environment. Work with environmental agencies or private firms to ensure safety and compliance. Engage in research that examines the impact of smells on environmental health.

Psychic and Spiritual Consulting: Offer readings or spiritual guidance based on the scents associated with individuals or locations. Work as a medium or psychic who specializes in interpreting scents that convey messages from the spiritual realm.

Therapy and Counseling: Use your superpower ability in therapy to explore and resolve emotional issues based on the scents associated with past experiences or traumas. Specialize in aroma-based therapy techniques to help clients manage stress, anxiety, and other conditions.

Forensic Analysis: Use your olfactory skills to help solve crimes. Work in forensic or criminal investigations to detect clues that others might miss. Collaborate with law enforcement agencies to provide insights that require acute scent detection.

Teaching and Education: Educate others about the use and benefits of Clairscent in fields like perfumery, therapy, and environmental science. Conduct workshops, and seminars, or create online courses focused on developing olfactory skills. Be a consultant for human resources to help hire the appropriate sensory smeller for specific jobs where they need that skillset.

Holistic and Alternative Medicine: Work to preserve traditional practices involving herbal medicine or naturopathy, where understanding scents can enhance the therapeutic use of herbs and natural remedies. Advise clients on lifestyle changes and wellness practices based on scents that positively impact their health by figuring out which scents they have an affinity or an aversion to.

Cultural Preservation and Anthropology: Work to preserve traditional practices involving scents, such as incense-making or the cultivation of aromatic plants. Research and document the role of scent in historical and cultural contexts.

These career paths leverage the unique abilities of individuals with Clairscent, enabling them to contribute meaningfully in diverse fields, from health and wellness to environmental and cultural preservation.

Detecting Clairscent in Others

Recognizing these superpower abilities in others can make interactions deeper and more meaningful. Here are ways you might understand someone with clear-smelling:

Observational Signs:

A person might answer questions or react to comments related to scents without these being mentioned, revealing that they communicate with the world through smells.

They smell things others don't mention or smell. When they ask if you smell it, they are shocked that you didn't. It is strong for them.

Watch how they describe things that seem random to you, but are identifiable to them through their heightened sense of smell.

Behavioral Indicators:

They speak of smelling things before they happen, such as predicting the scent of a meal before it is cooked or reacting to an aroma before it becomes noticeable to others.

A strong reaction to the common smells of someone's home, office, or cooking.

They may describe smelling distinct scents or aromas in their dreams that later become real, or share insights gained from olfactory dream experiences.

Communicating with a Clairscent Individual:

Be clear and speak about scents and fragrances and ask them what they sense or smell when going into a new environment or when you notice they are in the moment of their Clairscent.

Engage in discussions about metaphysical phenomena, including aromatherapy and scent-related phenomena, creating a supportive environment for them to share their clear-smelling experiences.

Acknowledge their experiences without judgment, encouraging open and honest communication about their scent insights.

Helping Others Understand Clairscent Messages:

Use language that is relatable and grounded. Instead of saying, "I smell strange scents," one might say, "I sense distinct smells", and ask if the person next to you smells them as well.

Give real examples of how Clairscent has given you beneficial insights in the past.

Teach others to recognize subtle clear-sense clues, which helps them relate to this superpower.

Present clear-smelling insights in a way that is relevant to real-world issues or decisions at hand.

Cultivating a Supportive Environment for Clairscent Individuals:

Explain what this sensory superpower is, clarifying any misconceptions. Educating others assists in demystifying this less commonly understood sensory ability is a great way to connect.

Honor personal boundaries when sharing or discussing these experiences. Ensure consent and comfort levels to support respectful and ethical interactions. If they want to hear, great, share, if they don't, just understand that they are not getting the same information you are.

Encourage healthy skepticism and critical to balance their understanding of these supernatural experiences.

Use this tool in teamwork, adding a new dimension to creative problem-solving. You don't have to explain all that you intuit, just share the information in a way that builds camaraderie.

Leveraging Clairscent Collaboratively:

Use people with this smelling superpower as a unique tool in team problem-solving. Scent-based insights can lead to fresh ideas, effective brainstorming, and better strategies.

Involve Clairscent people in creative projects. Their deep understanding of scents can add new dimensions to culinary arts, product development, and marketing strategies.

Always make sure to respect the privacy and emotional well-being of others.

Communicating with clear-scent people requires sensitivity and open-mindedness. By building trust and respect, these skills can be the bridge that connects you to personal and professional relationships, boosting a collaborative environment to instigate growth for all.

These practices not only improve team dynamics but also spark innovation, especially in industries related to fragrance, food, and beverages. This superpower can be key in resolving complex and giving deep insights into what customers want based on scent awareness.

Practical Exercises for Clairscent

Developing this superpower involves improving your ability to discern and perceive subtle smells. Here are some practical exercises to enhance your abilities:

Sensory Recall Practice: Select a variety of familiar scents and smell them one by one. After experiencing each scent, take a break and go to another area, then try to recall them in your mind. This strengthens your scent memory.

Concentrated Aroma Meditation: Choose an aroma, such as lavender, coffee, or citrus. Close your eyes, clear your mind, and try to imagine the scent in your mind without physically smelling it. This meditation develops your focus and ability to generate details while honing your Clairscent skills.

Blind Smelling Tests: With the help of a friend, conduct blind smelling tests using various scents. This sharpens your ability to discern subtle differences and nuances in scents.

Scent-to-Emotion Transformation: Smell different essential oils, herbs, or aromatic substances and try to connect these to emotional experiences. This practice helps bridge the connection between your sense of smell and emotional responses, improving your overall sensory superpower.

Journaling Olfactory Experiences: Keep a journal of the scents you notice throughout the day, and any feelings they bring. This helps you document and understand your Clairscent experiences and how you receive information personally.

Progressive Relaxation for Enhanced Sensitivity: Use muscle relaxation techniques while focusing on relaxing your nasal passages, sinuses, and respiratory system. Relaxing these specific areas can heighten sensitivity to scents.

Scent Pairing Visualization: Visualize combinations of scents and how they might interact with each other. Imagine how different scents mix and influence each other. This exercise boosts your creativity in scent blending.

Ethical Practice Reflections: Reflect regularly on the ethical implications of your scent superpower and how others are reacting around you. Keep a healthy boundary around how much you share and don't share and be sensitive to others. If you know something, they don't have to.

These exercises not only enhance clear-smelling abilities but also help you develop a deeper appreciation and understanding of how these unique sensory experiences can be integrated into your daily life and cause immense personal growth.

By dedicating time to these exercises and reflections, you can refine your clear-smelling abilities. This will enhance your intuitive abilities both with personal insight and professional sensitivity. This allows you to navigate complex scenarios and relationships with greater ease and depth. These practices not only strengthen your sensory smelling superpowers, they promote a mindful approach to the nuances of everyday life, bridging the gap between the seen and the unseen.

Progressive Training

Each exercise in this chapter builds on the one before it, starting with simple scent awareness and moving to more complex guided meditations that encourage deeper spiritual development. By practicing regularly, you'll not only improve your clear-smelling capabilities but also your overall spiritual awareness. The goal is to smell beyond the physical and to connect with the deeper information and intuition that this superpower can reveal.

By spending time on these exercises and meditations, you build a strong foundation for your sensory-smelling journey. This paves the way for deep insights and intuitive abilities. Remember that patience and consistency is key to unlocking the full potential of your psychic smell.

As you explore and develop your Clairscent abilities, it's essential to recognize their potential as a valuable tool for understanding and connecting with the world around you. By honing your skills, exercising discernment, and respecting ethical boundaries, you can harness the power of intuitive smelling to bring positive change to both your life and the lives of others. Embracing these abilities with gratitude and responsibility allows you to tap into a deeper layer of sensory perception, providing profound insights into the hidden cues of the world. This chapter not only aims to educate and inspire those interested in Clairscent but also encourages the integration of this extraordinary sense into a broader understanding of human capabilities.

By doing so, it fosters a deeper, more empathetic engagement with the intricate tapestry of life's aromas.

If you are eager to elevate your smelling abilities to discover your full potential, understand its applications, and achieve success in various aspects of your life, consider enrolling in a specialized course designed to help you master these skills. Sign up for the "Awakening Your Superpowers" class available at superpowersunleashed.com. This course is tailored to guide you through the nuances, helping you harness these abilities for personal growth and professional success. Take the step today to unlock your sensory superpowers and transform your approach to life's challenges and opportunities.

To further your exploration of mastering your smelling superpower and to connect with others who share your interests globally, refer to the Free Resources page to find out how you can be supported further.

As we continue this journey of uncovering your intuitive gifts, the next chapter will reveal Clairsentience, exploring how you can harness the power of touch and feeling to gain deeper insights and understanding. Let's embark on this new exploration together. Let's go!

CHAPTER 6:
THE EMPATHIC ART
Clairsentience

Welcome to the captivating world of Clairsentience, where you can sense and feel the invisible vibrations of the universe. This chapter will help you understand this superpower, illustrating how this extraordinary sense not only heightens your emotional awareness but also connects you to the deep, resonant energies that transcend time and space.

Clairsentience, or "clear feeling," is the special ability to sense and feel energies that most people can't. This includes detecting the emotions of others, sensing energy from objects and places, and picking up on emotional vibes from different times or dimensions. Unlike regular empathy, Clairsentience gives you more spiritual insights, warnings, or confirmations that aren't obvious to everyone.

To use this ability, start paying attention to the subtle signals your body and emotions send you. You might notice sudden temperature changes, tingling sensations, or unexplained emotions when you are around certain people or in new places. These experiences are not random; they are powerful messages intended to guide you through life. Early signs of Clairsentience can also include a strong sense of knowing or feeling about people or situations, often mistaken for intuition or gut feelings.

In everyday life, this superpower offers incredible advantages. It helps you understand and empathize in all relationships. By sensing the emotional undercurrents within someone's words, you can discern their true intentions and emotional states, guiding you to respond with greater compassion and effectiveness. This ability allows you to align with their unspoken emotional needs.

Developing this sensory ability involves awareness, meditation, and practice. Begin by paying close attention to your intuitive feelings, whether they are strong or subtle. Meditation helps quiet your mind, making it easier to understan the energies around you. Practicing mindfulness in daily interactions sharpens your skills, helping you notice both spoken and unspoken emotional cues.

As your clear-feeling abilities grow stronger, you will find yourself connecting with people and places on a deeper level. This connection offers comfort, guidance, and a profound sense of alignment with the flow of life.

Clairsentience gives you invaluable insights when making decisions. By tuning into these deeper emotional frequencies, you gain clarity and understanding, helping you make choices that are best for you. This guidance is especially useful during moments of emotional uncertainty or when navigating complex emotional feelings.

Embracing this feeling of superpower opens a gateway to a deeper understanding of the universe and your role in it. By learning to recognize and interpret subtle emotional signals, you gain knowledge that goes beyond normal senses. This chapter invites you to explore the rich tapestry of emotions, enriching your life with wisdom from your deep emotional awareness. It aims to help you understand Clairsentience, from recognizing its signs to using its insights in everyday life. By embracing the symphony of unseen emotions, you can experience life with heightened empathy and understanding, rooted in both the seen and unseen.

The concept of clear feeling has roots that are as ancient as human civilization, cultures, religions, and spiritual practices around the world. This amazing ability, lets people feel and sense energies beyond the physical senses have been both respected and feared, often surrounded by a sense of mystery and power.

Here is an Overview of the History of Clairsentience

In ancient civilizations, such as the shamans of Siberia, the oracles of Greece, and the seers of the Celtic tribes believed Clairsentience was a divine gift from the gods that provided insight into the unseen world of spirits and deities. These early intuitives were respected community advisors and healers. They could sense the emotional and spiritual needs of their people, and connect with the natural world on a deeply empathic level.

During the Middle Ages, the view of Clairsentience changed a lot because of the rise of organized religion. Sensitives, often labeled as mystics or heretics depending on the cultural context, either served under the protection of the church or were persecuted for their abilities. A good example of this is with Hildegard von Bingen and Joan of Arc, respected for their divine insights, however, even between these two women, one was celebrated and the other killed for heresy for having these insights. Joan of Arc was killed at the age of only 19 years old for heresy but was later canonized as a Saint in the Catholic Church. This period was challenging for Clairsentients because of the religious and political turmoil.

In the 19th century, Clairsentience became popular again with the Spiritualist movement in Europe and America. Mediums and psychics used their abilities to feel the presence of spirits and shared messages from the afterlife, often in sessions filled with eager participants seeking comfort or closure. This era brought Clairsentience into the public eye, making it a topic of both scientific curiosity and popular fascination.

In the 20th century, the study of this specific superpower expanded with the development of parapsychology. Researchers like J.B. Rhine at Duke University attempted to put psychic abilities, including Clairsentience, within a scientific framework. Psychology began to explore how people could be empathically attuned to others, sometimes close to what we call Clairsentience.

Today, Clairsentience is often discussed in New Age and spiritual practices where it is seen as a path to gain deeper self-awareness and connect with the universe. It is frequently used in holistic healing practices, such as Reiki and energy work, where practitioners use their empathic abilities to detect and balance the energy flows in the body.

As humanity progresses into a future where the lines between science and spirituality continue to blur, the understanding and acceptance of Clairsentience are likely to grow. With advances in neuroscience and sophisticated studies of human consciousness, Clairsentience might one day be fully understood not just as a psychic phenomenon but as an advanced form of human empathy and intuition.

The history of Clairsentience is a testament to the human ability to sense the world beyond the physical. As both an art and a science, it challenges us to consider the depths of human perception and the potential of truly feeling the world around us.

Historical Figure in Clairsentience

A historical figure known for his Clairsentient abilities is Emanuel Swedenborg. Born in 1688 in Sweden, Swedenborg was a scientist, philosopher, theologian, and mystic whose extensive writings often talk about detailed spiritual experiences and perceptions.

Swedenborg began his career as a scientist and inventor. However, in his mid-fifties, he experienced a powerful spiritual awakening. He claimed that this awakening opened his senses to the spiritual world, allowing him to communicate with angels, demons, and other spiritual beings. He described in detail the afterlife and the spiritual dimensions connected to different human emotions.

What sets Swedenborg apart as a Clairsentient is his detailed descriptions of feeling the emotional and spiritual states of the deceased and angels. He wrote a lot about his experiences in his books "Heaven and Hell" and "Arcana Coelestia". His ability to feel and understand these spiritual messages was key to his theological and philosophical work. This influenced many later thinkers and writers, including William Blake, Ralph Waldo Emerson, and Carl Jung.

Swedenborg's detailed accounts of his spiritual experiences and his interpretations of Christian theology through his Clairsentient insights had a significant impact on religious thought. This led to the creation of the New Church (or Swedenborgianism), a new Christian denomination based on his teachings.

His work remains a fascinating case study in the history of mysticism and clear-feeling, offering a unique view on the human ability to perceive beyond the physical senses into the emotional and spiritual realms.

Where is Clairsentience Located?

Clairsentience isn't located in a specific place in the body like our traditional senses are. Instead, it's connected to the body's entire sensory and emotional system. Clairsentience involves being very sensitive to the energies and emotions around you, which can show up as physical sensations or feelings.

Many people who identify as Clairsentient report feeling sensations in their solar plexus, the area around the stomach. This is often called the "gut feeling" area, believed to be closely linked to intuition. The solar plexus is considered a center of personal power and emotional intelligence in many spiritual traditions.

The heart is another important center of intuitive perception, especially related to feelings. You may feel warmth, openness, or tightness in response to feeling the emotions of yourself and others.

Even though this superpower is more commonly associated with Clairvoyance or "clear seeing," the third eye, located on the forehead between the eyebrows, is also thought to be a center where Clairsentients can feel certain sensations related to their abilities, such as pressure, tingling, or a sense of knowing.

From a psychological point of view, Clairsentience can also be experienced as a heightened state of empathy, where your brain's mirror neurons (which help you feel empathy and understand others' emotions), are very active. This means this superpower isn't located in one part specifically but involves multiple areas of the brain responsible for emotions and sensory processing.

In short, while you might experience this clear-feeling superpower through different sensations in the body, it does not have a fixed physical location as mentioned. This sense is a more holistic sense involving much more of the body and mind's interconnected emotional and sensory systems.

Common Beginnings of Clairsentience

1. **Spontaneous Sensations:** Many people with Clairsentient abilities feel unexpected physical or emotional sensations without any clear cause. These experiences can happen when awake or in dreams and might include sudden chills, feelings of warmth, or

emotional surges linked to past events or unknown reasons.

2. **Peripheral Sensory Phenomena:** Clairsentients can pick up on feelings or energies that seem to come from the periphery of their awareness, adding an extra layer to their senses. These can be sudden feelings of unease, joy, or sadness that disappear when focused on, initially confusing but later recognized as genuine Clairsentient signs.

3. **Childhood Experiences:** Like many intuitive abilities, Clairsentience often appears in early childhood. Kids may show an unusual awareness of others' feelings or describe sensations that they shouldn't logically know about, such as the presence of a deceased relative or the emotions of a distant family member.

4. **Heightened Empathy:** People with clear-feeling superpowers typically have a strong sensitivity to the emotions and energies around them. This enhanced empathy lets them 'feel' beyond the surface interactions, often sensing the underlying moods or intentions of others even when not spoken aloud.

5. **Trigger Events:** Significant life events with traumatic events, such as accidents, severe illnesses, or emotional

losses, can awaken or intensify these abilities. These profound experiences often shift one's perceptual boundaries, opening them up to deeper sensory and emotional layers.

6. **Environmental Echoes:** Some Clairsentients find that their sensitivity is triggered or heightened by certain environments. The vibe of a historical site, the energy of a crowded room, or the calm of nature can trigger deeper sensory experiences, linking them directly with the broader emotional landscape.

7. **Chemical or Material Sensitivity:** Exposure to specific chemicals or materials can sometimes spark Clairsentient experiences. People might feel unusual sensations or emotions in urban settings or when in contact with new synthetic substances.

8. **Meditative and Spiritual Practices:** Practicing regular meditation, prayer, or other spiritual practices can significantly develop Clairsentient abilities. These practices help quiet the mind and increase sensitivity to subtle energies and emotions usually hidden by daily distractions.

9. **Cultural and Ritualistic Practices:** In various cultures, traditional practices involving sacred rituals can increase clear-feeling experiences. Participating in

these rituals often creates a deeper emotional connection, making spiritual or emotional messages more accessible.

10. **Amplified Sensitivity in Social Settings**: Clairsentients may notice underlying emotions or energies in social environments that others miss. This often shows up as a strong awareness of the mood in a room, the true intentions behind people's words, or the emotional history of a place.

11. **Sudden Awareness in Charged Environments:** Clairsentients often recognize their abilities in situations where emotions run high, such as heated meetings or family gatherings. They may pick up on subtle emotional undercurrents or sense the overall energy of the environment, providing them with insights others might miss.

Understanding these common beginnings can help you recognize and develop your Clairsentient abilities, integrating them into your daily lives for better interactions and deeper personal insight.

Signs of Emerging Clairsentience

Clear-feeling is an extrasensory ability that lets people sense and feel energies and emotions without any direct physical interaction. This ability connects deeply with the spiritual and energetic layers where the physical and metaphysical worlds intersect. Here's how it works:

1. **How Clear-Feeling Works:** This sensory superpower uses the body's emotional and physical response systems. Unlike taste, used in Clairgustance, Clairsentience mainly uses the body's sensory and empathic channels to receive information. Sensitives may feel things like tingling, warmth, or pressure, or have emotional impressions that seem to come from nowhere, often from the non-physical realm.

2. **Connection with the Nervous System:** People who experience this sensory ability might feel sudden mood changes or emotional states triggered by memories, environments, or unseen energies. These feelings aren't always linked to immediate causes, suggesting that this ability uses unique pathways in the nervous system to connect to emotional and energetic awareness.

3. **Psychic and Spiritual Connection:** This superpower is closely connected to both psychic and spiritual dimensions, often allowing people to receive intuitive messages or emotional insights from spiritual guides, the collective consciousness, or the energy of places and people. For example, a sudden feeling of

calm might indicate spiritual protection or guidance, while unease might signal a warning.

4. **Emotional and Energetic Resonance:** The feelings sensed through clear-feeling can evoke strong emotional reactions and are closely linked to the energy of a person or a place. For example, you might feel overwhelmed with sadness in an area where a tragic event happened or feel unexplained joy around someone who is deeply content and peaceful. This can also spontaneously happen when you meet someone, you can feel an overwhelming feeling of love and connection and that you know them, or you could feel a distinct aversion and a feeling of not wanting to be around someone at all. This is because you are picking up on things that are nonphysical in cues.

5. **Practical Uses:** This superpower can be invaluable in fields such as counseling, psychic readings, or healing practices. Therapists might use Clairsentient abilities to better understand and address their clients' emotional needs, while psychics may interpret these sensations to give guidance to others. In healing modalities, sensing energy flow and blockages can guide the healing process.

6. **Development Clairsentience:** Like other psychic abilities, this sensory superpower can be developed through awareness, practice, and meditation. Techniques to enhance Clairsentience might include focusing on body sensations and emotional responses during meditation, clearing emotional channels to receive subtler energies, or using grounding practices to manage and understand psychic sensations better.

Understanding this superpower involves recognizing its amazing connection to our physical senses and deeper metaphysical insights. It transcends ordinary emotional experiences, offering a unique perspective on the energies around us. By developing this ability, you can deepen your understanding of the world, enhance interactions with others, and connect more deeply with the unseen energies in your environment. Embracing Clairsentience promises to enrich your engagement with both the visible and the invisible aspects of life.

Signs You Have Clairsentience

As said earlier, clear-feeling is a superpower ability to sense and understand the emotional and energetic cues around you. This skill goes beyond ordinary senses and taps into subtle energies and emotions. Here are some of the experiences commonly associated with Clairsentience:

1. **Emotional Echoes:** Feeling sudden, unexplainable emotions such as sadness, joy, or anxiety that aren't yours. They belong to people or places around you.
2. **Precognitive Sensations**: Having physical sensations or emotions about events before they happen, such as a sense of foreboding or excitement. Very often in the news when people have been attacked in public places, they often refer to the feeling that they knew not to go to their car, or down that alley. They picked up on something in this sensory superpower within.
3. **Empathic Resonance:** Sensing the emotions and physical feelings of others as if they were your own, even if you aren't close to them. Twins often sense this, but clear-feeling and empaths can feel this even without that connection.
4. **Aura Detection:** Perceiving the emotional or energetic auras around people, animals, or objects, that others can't detect.
5. **Spiritual Communications:** Feeling sensations or emotions connected with spiritual entities, guides, or deceased loved ones. This could be suddenly thinking of

someone that you love who passed and feeling sadness, joy, or smiling over the thought of them.

6. **Symbolic Sensations:** Experiencing physical sensations in dreams or visions that carry messages or foretell future events. This could be an overwhelming feeling when you awaken from a dream, that this was real and you question if it was just a dream.

7. **Peripheral Awareness:** Detecting subtle shifts in energy that seem to arise spontaneously or from nowhere. Anything that suddenly breaks up the natural flow of where you are and what you are doing is experiencing Clairsentience.

8. **Chakra Activations:** Experiencing sudden tingling, warmth, or pressure in areas related to the body's chakras, particularly around the stomach or heart. You might be introduced to something in your daily life, that connects with another lifetime and the memory of it is coming through and into your reality, without you understanding exactly what it is. Or, this could be an activation because it's time for you to read that specific energy of something that you are either being introduced to or something spontaneously happening in the non-physical.

9. **Sudden Insights:** Receiving clear emotional or physical insights into problems or situations without a logical reason. You might be picking up on something going on within the other person, such as when they are about to eat something, you can sense what their bodily reaction is going to be before they take a bite.

10. **Pattern Recognition:** Noticing emotional or energetic patterns that seem to convey important messages or warnings. You are more than equipped with this ability to sense much deeper and more poignant messages and they happen spontaneously.

11. **Déjà Felt:** Feeling as though you have previously experienced a specific emotional or physical sensation. This can be as mentioned in another sensory ability, even knowing what one person is going to say and what is going to happen. They suddenly come into your awareness, and then after a short while, suddenly disappear.

12. **Vivid Emotional Dreams:** Having emotionally intense dreams that provide information about personal or external future events. People often discount these, and it's important to honor that you are experiencing this for a specific reason. Ask what that is, so that you can receive the benefit of it.

13. **Residual Feelings:** Feeling lingering emotions or energies in specific places that offer insights into past events or the emotional states of previous occupants. I have experienced this many times while visiting sites like The Ghetto in The Czech Republic. I felt dizzy after getting off the tour bus and had to readjust my ability to sense emotions stuck in that space, to go on my way and see the area.

14. **Intuitive Empathy:** Developing a deep, intuitive understanding of others' feelings and emotional conditions beyond what they see. Being careful of noticing this without taking on the energy is paramount to your well-being.

15. **Energetic Sensitivity:** Sensing emotional or energetic awareness in environments that carry significant emotional residues. This could be from something someone else experienced, or coming from a repressed memory of something in your past.

16. **Gut Reactions:** Strong, gut feelings that guide decision-making or warn about people or situations. This often is the sudden feeling of the need to do something, or not do something.

17. **Natural Empathy:** A strong, innate ability to connect with others' emotions, often leading to roles in

caregiving, therapy, or other empathic professions. It is highly recommended to consider if you are being called to assist, or doing a knee-jerk, "I have to help this person because I know it" reaction.

18. **Spontaneous Understanding:** Suddenly understanding complex emotional states or the dynamics between people, conveyed through subtle energetic exchanges. This is beneficial when wanting to assist or guide others in conflict resolution.

19. **Accurate Emotional Forecasts:** Being able to predict how situations will unfold based on the emotional cues perceived. These are special cues for you to use to discern what actions to take.

20. **Symbolic Language of Emotions:** Intuitively understanding the deeper meanings of the emotional or energetic cues. Honing that skill helps use your discernment.

21. **Receiving Guidance:** Feeling as though specific emotional advice or insights are communicated directly to you, especially regarding personal or relational issues. This is typically by cues your body is giving you in certain places, such as everyone that I've spoken with, has their cue of confirmations, could be chills running down the body, or something specific that

happens only to that person to let them know it's a yes or a no.

22. **Sensitivity to Energy Shifts:** Being very aware of energy shifts in the environment, felt as emotional or physical sensations.

23. **Emotional Synchronicities:** Experiencing frequent emotional coincidences that can be great to guide your decisions or relationships.

24. **Affirmations from Emotions:** Getting confirmations through emotional responses that validate your thoughts, feelings, or questions. This could be from you or others.

These signs of Clairsentience can show up as emotional or physical sensations or as a deep-seated connection to the energies around you. It's crucial to consider that Clairsentience is very personal, and its signs can vary widely in intensity and frequency according to how developed your clear-sensing abilities are.

People who experience these signs often describe them as intermittent and initially outside their control. It is wise to further develop them through practices such as meditation, energy work, and guidance from experts who can assist in identifying them for you and helping you understand your specific sensitivities.

Real Examples of Clairsentience

From an early age, my ability to sense and absorb the emotional energies of others was strikingly clear. An incident, at the age of only 13 started shaping my understanding of Clairsentience. One day, a friend of mine called and I had been in a cheerful mood, but as she vented, I found myself feeling her feelings instead of my own. This sudden change of how I felt, was swift and distinct. I knew my day had changed and didn't understand. Once I helped guide her to better feelings and relief, she hung up and I was left with a feeling of anger and wanting to slit my wrist. I was bewildered and knew to ask for help.

Very often when I needed extra guidance as a child, I would walk outside and ask questions that I needed answers to. I asked why I suddenly felt like a different person when I had been in a great mood beforehand. The intuition that I received was a profound one. I was given the download about how I had taken on the energy of my friend, instead of just listening, I had felt it so strongly that I was now carrying it and she was relieved that she wasn't feeling it anymore. We exchanged energy.

This is a precarious thing for Clairsentients to experience and isn't something I recommend at all. I was given at that tender age, how to wipe off the energy of my friend off my body so that I would no longer carry the emotions and anger. The process was to take my right hand and put it on top of my left shoulder wipe down my arm and then repeat on the other side with my left hand onto my right shoulder, saying that I chose not to carry the energy of my friend anymore.

Once I did that, the emotions that had been deflected onto me suddenly disappeared and I was left in a whole new world of understanding the importance of not taking on the energy of others. I struggled with this for years, until I got proficient at it. My abilities to read and sense things in school led to me being called "The Counselor" in Jr. High and High School. Kids were coming to me for support and guidance and things suddenly got better in their lives because of what I sensed and shared that would help them.

This is something intrinsically important that I do for clients who have these sensitivities. Knowing how you process things, how you receive them, and how you communicate with them are paramount to your well-being in life. Once you know these things, you can then make decisions that are in alignment with what is the highest good for you and, thus others.

Many years later, this lesson proved crucial during an encounter with a client in my car. As we left the parking lot of the restaurant, where we had enjoyed a nice meal, a man in a large SUV aggressively sped past us, and swerved in front of me, going more than 30 mph over the speed limit I immediately detected his hostility toward me and began to see a ball of energy coming from his vehicle. Using clairsentience and clairvoyance, I could feel and see the anger coming at us. I stopped the conversation with my client who was asking me questions, to address this encounter head-on. I explained to her in real time what was happening with the negative energy approaching from the man and told her what he had recently gone through and why he was so angry at women, therefore his projection onto me as a female driver.

I also explained to her about not taking on the energy of others, for what he was feeling or why, was none of my business, and how to return to sender, that which didn't belong to me. As I spoke, she began to understand, but couldn't see what was transpiring and mentioned that she wished she could see it.

I asked Spirit to allow her to see this phenomenon as it was happening. The ball of energy kept getting closer to our car. Her clairvoyant ability opened, as I had requested and she began to see the ball of energy getting bigger by the second coming at us. She froze.

I explained quickly that instead of allowing us to take on the negative energy he was projecting, I was going to return the energy to him so that he could heal whatever this was about and that it was none of my business because I had nothing to do with his anger. And, that she would see the ball of energy go back to his vehicle with a noticeable hit. I explained that my actions were about loving him unconditionally by letting him carry what was making him angry and that he could heal it within if he became aware of it.

Just before the energy enveloped us, I said aloud that I returned the energy to the sender and told him that I did this with love for him. The energy immediately flipped with a beautiful curve and went straight back to his vehicle. As the energy hit his car, the man swerved off the road a little. He began to slow his car down significantly.

I glanced over at my client to check on her, only to find her looking as pale as a ghost, her mouth hanging open in shock. She couldn't believe what she had just witnessed and admitted that she wondered if I was going to let that negative energy affect us. It was a valuable moment to teach her firsthand about the impact of others projecting energy onto innocent people, how to protect ourselves from it, and the importance of using our superpowers to make wise choices in life by embracing our abilities.

Another poignant example of a clear feeler involves a different client who had begun to isolate herself due to the overwhelming emotional pain and suffering she felt in public spaces. In a session, she began to realize that she had a heightened Clairsentient ability and was unconsciously feeling the thoughts and emotions of others and would go home and become despondent, not wanting to go out, wanting to hide and not feel. She began to understand why she wanted to hide so that she could feel safe in her own space and avoid interactions with others. This was ultimately hurting her because as humans, we all need to connect and share our lives with others. That secluding herself wasn't for her highest good.

As she became aware of how much having Clairsentience had impacted her and that there were choices she could make before going out in public, she started to heal the pain she had felt her entire life. By helping her understand who she was, how she naturally communicated with the world with this special sensory superpower, and how she could manage it, the pain of having it became the joy of using it. She learned to get the information she needed and how to use it for her own good. She started going out in public and even started dating again. She learned to trust her instincts, which is one of the greatest benefits of this ability. We talked in another session later, about how her life had changed before and after understanding who she was and how she now used her abilities with ease. By helping her learn how to handle this special sensory ability, she turned her life from loneliness to connection with others.

These experiences highlight the commonality and intensity of Clairsentient encounters in the world of those highly sensitive to energies. Throughout thousands of sessions, I've observed that everyone possesses some level of Clairsentience. This innate ability serves as a crucial indicator of alignment with our surroundings and decisions. Teaching individuals to manage, rather than be overwhelmed by this sensitivity, enables them to harness their unique abilities for personal growth and a better understanding of their environment.

This ability is part of the innate intelligence within that is our inner guidance system wanting to communicate with us, give us the information that we need, and the discernment to make decisions that are clear and useful.

Benefits of Clairsentience in Communication

In Relationships:

Clairsentience greatly improves communication by allowing you a deeper understanding of others beyond words. The ability to feel someone's emotional energy or the 'vibe' gives you a unique advantage in all relationships.

A Clairsentient person has an innate knowledge of the emotions and intentions behind what people say. This empathic intelligence helps you respond with compassion and understanding, deepening connections and making relationships more meaningful.

By sensing potential misunderstandings or emotional conflicts, a Clairsentient can address issues before they become bigger problems, promoting harmony in relationships.

Feeling things from the perspective of another fosters empathy and understanding, allowing for more supportive and nurturing relationships.

In Monetizing:

In business, Clairsentience can be monetized by making strategic decisions based on insights into emotional undercurrents, team dynamics, and competitive mindsets that others might miss.

People who possess this feeling superpower can offer their services to individuals or businesses to guide them in personal life decisions or business strategies. This makes you a valuable consultant to others because of your ability to discern and interpret emotional cues.

With the ability to feel the unspoken, negotiations can be navigated with a level of foresight, ensuring better outcomes and financial gains.

Getting Clarity on Others:

Discerning the true intentions and emotions of others can protect against deception, ensuring trust in both personal and professional relationships.

Understanding the specific emotional needs and preferences of others allows for more effective and appreciated communication. You can reach people on a deeper level, which makes them want to be around you and do business with you.

Cultivating Clairsentience for Growth:

Regularly practicing mindfulness and sensitivity exercises can enhance Clairsentience, allowing for clearer and more accurate emotional awareness.

Sharing insights with others and getting feedback can refine your ability to interpret clear-feeling information correctly.

Engaging with books and courses on Clairsentience and spiritual development can provide tools and techniques to better harness this ability.

Enhancing Your Clairsentient Abilities:

Incorporate daily exercises that boost your emotional awareness and enhance your ability to detect and interpret the feelings you sense from others.

Engage in meditations that focus on experiencing and understanding a wide range of emotional states. This can heighten your sensitivity and responsiveness to your emotional cues.

Connect with groups or communities dedicated to psychic and intuitive development. Sharing experiences and learning from others can provide valuable support and accelerate your personal growth.

By integrating these methods into your routine, you can significantly enhance your clear-feeling abilities. This not only enriches your relationships but also creates new opportunities for financial success.

Potential Challenges of Clairsentience if Mismanaged or Unrecognized

Having this sensory superpower can introduce a unique set of challenges and issues that might affect people who possess or develop these abilities. Here are some potential issues that Clairsentients may face:

1. Receiving constant or intense clear-feeling information can be overwhelming, leading to sensory overload or mental exhaustion.
2. Clairsentients might sometimes find it challenging to differentiate between the energies they feel and the

physical reality, which can be disorienting or lead to confusion.

3. Feeling the emotions associated with others' experiences or locations can have a profound emotional impact and may lead to anxiety, fear, or feeling the need to isolate oneself.
4. These superpowers might unintentionally access sensitive emotional information about others, leading to ethical concerns about privacy.
5. There is a risk of misinterpreting clear-feeling insights, which can result in making incorrect decisions or spreading misinformation.
6. Facing skepticism or disbelief from others can lead to feelings of isolation or self-doubt.
7. There may be social stigma attached to this sensory ability, which can affect personal and professional relationships and lead to social isolation.
8. Clairsentients may question their mental health when beginning to experience unexplained phenomena, due to fear of being seen as delusional or mentally unstable.
9. Some report physical symptoms associated with heightened feeling experiences, such as headaches or fatigue from energy overload.

10. Friends and family might struggle to understand or accept the Clairsentient's experiences, which can strain or complicate relationships.
11. They may find it hard to set and maintain emotional boundaries, leading to emotional entanglement or a feeling of intrusion.
12. Handling the information gained through this feeling superpower requires ethical considerations about when and how to share it.
13. Focusing too much on the feelings of others can distract from living in the present moment and handling immediate, practical aspects of life.
14. Others might have unrealistic expectations of Clairsentient abilities, assuming they are infallible or can solve all problems, causing unnecessary stress or pressure.
15. Often, clear-feelers use their ability to sense energies for others but neglect to use them for their personal decisions. Recognizing and using these abilities for personal benefits and growth is the highest use of this superpower.
16. Clairsentients often struggle with discerning whether the energies and emotions they feel are their own or

picked up from others. This can create confusion and difficulty in understanding one's feelings.

People with these sensory feeling superpowers often benefit from learning how to manage their abilities and find balance. This can involve setting healthy boundaries, developing coping strategies, and seeking support from understanding communities. Guidance from a more experienced Clairsentient can help them understand their abilities and use them for personal and professional success in life.

Career Paths for Clairsentients

The ability to intuitively sense and feel the emotional and energetic states of others and your environment can be a valuable skill in many professional positions. Here are several career paths that can be great for people with Clairsentient abilities:

Counseling and Therapy: Clairsentients have a natural ability to understand and empathize with others' emotions, making careers in counseling or psychotherapy a great fit. They can use their empathic abilities to connect deeply with clients and provide insights into clients' feelings and behaviors that might not otherwise be obvious to the client.

Energy Healing and Alternative Medicine: Careers in energy healing practices can benefit from Clairsentience. Practitioners can feel energy blockages or emotional disturbances in their clients and tailor their treatments to address these issues more effectively.

Spiritual Coaching and Mentoring: As spiritual coaches or mentors, Clairsentients can guide others on their spiritual journeys, offering deep emotional insights and support. They can help clients grow personally, understand their life purposes, or navigate spiritual awakenings.

Human Resources and Conflict Resolution: In human resources, clear-feelers can utilize their abilities to sense team dynamics and undercurrents. This skill is invaluable in resolving conflicts, managing team dynamics, and creating a harmonious workplace environment.

Artistic Careers: Artists, writers, and musicians with these sensory superpowers can use their deep emotional insights to create resonant and expressive work. Their ability to tap into and convey complex emotions can enhance their art and connect deeply with audiences.

Psychic and Intuitive Readings: Clairsentients can work as psychics or intuitive readers, using their abilities to provide guidance and clarity to those seeking help. Their capacity to feel and interpret energies can be useful in giving meaningful advice and foresight.

Social Work and Community Service: People with these superpowers are well-suited to social work, where they can use their empathetic abilities to help those in crisis or need. Their ability to understand and feel the emotions of others can provide support, advocacy, and solutions to individuals and communities.

Law Enforcement and Investigative Work: In law enforcement or private investigations, Clairsentients can sense the emotional truth behind people's statements or feel the atmosphere of a scene guiding investigations and helping in profiling or interrogations.

Education and Training: Educators and trainers with these heightened feeling abilities can understand and respond to the emotional and educational needs of their students. This sensitivity allows for a more adaptive teaching style that can address students' emotional and learning challenges.

Customer Service and Public Relations: In customer service and public relations, clear-feelers can excel by understanding and managing clients' emotions and expectations effectively. This can lead to improved customer satisfaction and loyalty.

Each of these career paths allows Clairsentients to use their natural empathic and intuitive strengths to make a meaningful impact in their careers and the lives of those they serve.

Detecting Clairsentience in Others

Recognizing Clairsentient abilities in others can lead to deeper interactions and better understanding. Here's how you might detect Clairsentience in others:

Observational Signs:

1. A person might react emotionally to conversations or situations without any visible cues, indicating they've sensed emotions or energies that haven't been mentioned.
2. They may seem to react to energies or emotions that aren't physically present as if sensing the mood or atmosphere that others cannot perceive.

3. Notice if they often seem to react to the emotional or energetic changes in an environment that are not apparent to others, catching subtle shifts that aren't obvious.
4. Clairsentients may seem to 'take on' the emotions of others around them, quickly shifting from one emotional state to another depending on their environment.
5. Notice if they experience physical symptoms (like goosebumps, stomachaches, or headaches) in response to intense emotional situations or environments, which is a sign of their heightened sensitivity.
6. They might frequently express having a "gut feeling" about situations or people that prove to be correct, reflecting their deep intuitive connection to their surroundings.

Behavioral Indicators:

1. They might express feelings or reactions to events before they happen, such as anticipating the emotional outcome of a meeting or personal interaction.
2. They have strong responses to the emotional tone in someone's communication, even when the words are neutral.

3. They might discuss feeling intense emotions or experiencing vivid interactions in their dreams that later come true, or share insights gained from dream experiences.
4. Due to their sensitivity to overwhelming energies, Clairsentients might avoid crowded or noisy environments where emotional and energetic stimuli are intense.
5. Often, Clairsentients are deeply compassionate, driven by the profound emotional insights they gain from others, making them naturally empathetic and caring.
6. They frequently find themselves in the role of an advisor or counselor, as others are drawn to their empathetic and understanding nature and benefit from monitoring how much service they give to nurture themselves.

Communicating With a Clairsentient Individual:

Be clear and straightforward in your interactions. Clairsentients may pick up on the emotional undertones of your words or the subtle implications behind your statements.

Engage in discussions about emotions, energies, and intuitive experiences, creating a supportive environment for them to share their insights.

Validate their experiences without judgment, encouraging open and honest communication about their intuitive awareness.

Since Clairsentients can pick up on subtle cues and underlying meanings, it's important to communicate with intention and awareness to avoid misunderstandings.

Being emotionally honest is crucial as clear-feelers can detect differences between what is said and what is felt, making transparency key to building trust.

Understand and respect their need for personal space and boundaries, as they can become overwhelmed by too much emotional input.

Offer support and understanding for their experiences. Acknowledging and validating their feelings helps them feel secure and valued.

By understanding these signs and knowing how to communicate effectively with Clairsentients, you can create a more empathetic and supportive connection, enabling them to feel understood and valued for their unique abilities.

Cultivating a Supportive Environment for Clairsentience:

Creating a nurturing environment for people with these sensory superpowers involves understanding and integrating their unique abilities in ways that enhance both personal and professional interactions. Here's how to cultivate a relationship that respects and leverages Clairsentience effectively:

Recognize and respect their ability to sense and feel energies. Validation can help build confidence and trust in their abilities.

Create an atmosphere where Clairsentients feel comfortable sharing their experiences and insights without fear of judgment. Open dialogue promotes mutual understanding and growth.

Be mindful of the emotional sensitivities. Offer support and understanding when they are overwhelmed by the energies they perceive.

Designate areas for quiet reflection and meditation. A serene environment can help Clairsentients tune into their abilities more effectively and manage sensory overload.

Provide access to books, workshops, and courses on Clairsentience and spiritual development to enhance their skills and understanding.

Suggest activities such as yoga, walking in nature, or mindfulness exercises to help them stay grounded and balanced amidst the energies they feel.

Emphasize the importance of using Clairsentient abilities ethically, respecting privacy, and maintaining personal boundaries.

Provide thorough explanations about what Clairsentience is, correcting any misconceptions. Educating others helps demystify this sensory ability, making it easier for them to be understood and accepted.

It is crucial to respect personal boundaries when engaging with Clairsentients. Prioritize obtaining consent and maintaining comfort levels to ensure respectful and ethical interactions. This not only protects privacy but also builds trust, essential for Clairsentients to feel secure in sharing their insights.

Encourage skepticism and critical analysis among peers and colleagues. This approach helps validate Clairsentient experiences and fosters a more grounded and objective understanding of these abilities.

By implementing these strategies, you can create a supportive and empowering environment for Clairsentients, enabling them to thrive both personally and professionally.

Leveraging Clairsentience Collaboratively

Utilize Clairsentience as a strategic tool in team problem-solving scenarios. They can sense underlying emotional currents and unspoken concerns that, lead to more effective and innovative solutions.

Leverage the unique emotional insights of people with these sensory superpowers in creative endeavors, such as arts, design, and human resources. Their ability to connect with and express deep emotional states can bring authenticity and depth to creative projects.

Ensure that these abilities are used ethically, respecting others' privacy and emotional well-being. People would benefit from managing their insights with discretion and integrity to avoid unintended harm.

Communication with clear-feelers with sensitivity to their perceptions and an openness to the non-verbal information they provide. Fostering an environment of mutual respect and understanding helps integrate these skills into personal relationships and professional teams.

Understanding the challenges faced by clear-feelers, such as sensory overload and difficulty distinguishing personal emotions from those of others, is crucial. Providing appropriate support and accommodations can help manage these issues, enhancing their well-being and effectiveness.

By promoting these practices, you can better interact with Clairsentients nurturing a relationship that benefits from a deeper mutual understanding and respect. This not only enhances the personal growth of the clear-feeler but also enriches the collective experience, making for a more empathetic and connected community or workplace.

Practical Exercises for Clairsentients

Developing your sensory feeling superpower involves enhancing your ability to discern and understand subtle emotional and energetic cues. Here are practical exercises designed to refine your Clairsentients:

Sensory Recall Practice: Take quiet moments to recall and feel emotions from the day or specific events, without any external triggers. This enhances your memory for emotional contexts and strengthens your ability to recall specific feelings. You may be surprised at how much information you gathered by feeling them.

Concentrated Emotion Meditation: Choose an emotion such as joy, sadness, or anger. Close your eyes, clear your mind, and try to feel this emotion within yourself without any external cause. This helps develop your focus and ability to generate detailed emotional perceptions internally.

Blind Empathy Testing: With a friend, conduct blind tests where they share a story or recall an emotion without revealing its context. Try to identify the emotions based solely on the energy you feel. This sharpens your empathic abilities and builds your capacity to discern subtle emotional nuances.

Aroma-to-Emotion Technique: Smell various herbs, spices, or other aromatic substances and try to connect these aromas with the specific emotions they invoke. This practice bridges the connection between Clairscent and Clairsentience.

Journaling Emotional Profiles: Keep a journal of the emotions you perceive throughout the day, both physical and those sensed through clear-feeling. Note any physical sensations associated with these emotions. This helps in documenting and making sense of your experiences, and recognizing patterns or triggers.

Progressive Relaxation for Enhanced Sensitivity: Engage in progressive muscle relaxation techniques while focusing on relaxing areas typically tense during emotional stress (e.g., jaw, shoulders). Relaxing these specific areas heightens your sensitivity to emotional cues, allowing for clearer feeling experiences.

Emotion Pairing Visualization: Visualize different scenarios and imagine the emotional reactions they would elicit. Consider how various situations might affect you or others emotionally. This promotes creativity in emotional understanding and enhances predictive Clairsentient abilities.

Ethical Practice Reflections: Reflect regularly on the ethical implications of your Clairsentient experiences, especially in terms of privacy and personal boundaries. This helps you maintain ethical practices ensuring respect for others' boundaries and personal integrity.

Daily Sensory Reflections: Each day, write down three things you sensed, noting whether these emotions or energies belonged to you or if you absorbed them from others. Reflect on whether you felt compelled to act on these feelings. This practice helps you discern between personal emotions and those picked up from external sources and maintain focus on personal emotional health.

These exercises not only enhance your superpower abilities but also help you integrate these unique sensory experiences into your daily life and personal growth. By dedicating time to these exercises and meditations, you lay a strong foundation for your Clairsentient journey, paving the way for profound insights and enhanced intuitive capabilities.

As we conclude this chapter on harnessing and developing your Clairsentient abilities, remember that the journey to mastering this profound sensory superpower is both enriching and deeply personal. With practice and dedication to the exercises outlined above, you can unlock greater depths of emotional and energetic perception, creating your understanding of yourself and the world around you. If you're curious about how you might already be using your Clairsentient abilities or wish to explore further how to refine and integrate these skills into your daily life, I invite you to schedule a discovery call with me. See the free resource page to learn how. This is a wonderful opportunity to delve deeper into your sensory experiences and to learn how you can harness your natural gifts to lead a more discerning, insightful, and fulfilling life.

Now that we've covered all of the top five senses/Clairs, let's look at how we can Own Our Genius by embracing who we are, and why we came into this world, and having fun while doing it. Identifying and monetizing your unique abilities is a journey of self-discovery and empowerment. It's about recognizing the incredible gifts you possess and using them to create a life filled with purpose, joy, and connection.

By understanding and developing your Clairs, you unlock a deeper level of awareness and intuition that guides you through life's challenges and opportunities. Celebrate your journey, trust in your abilities, and remember that the path to owning your genius is not only transformative but also a delightful adventure. Let's embark on this journey together, embracing our true selves and the boundless possibilities that lie ahead.

CHAPTER 7:
OWNING YOUR GENIUS

As we conclude this amazing and transformative journey, I want to thank you for exploring this path of self-discovery with me. Throughout this book, we have explored and uncovered your superpower abilities showing the unique genius within you. I hope you have discovered that learning who you truly are is the most empowering gift you can give to yourself and the world. The insights and tools shared here are meant to help you recognize and harness your sensory superpowers, allowing you to live a life of purpose, impact, and fulfillment. Thank you for your openness, dedication, and willingness to explore the extraordinary parts of you.

This journey does not end here—it is a continuous unfolding of your potential. Embrace every moment, trust in your intuitive abilities, and know that you are supported every step of the way. This book is a beginning, not an end. It is a guide to help you unlock and explore the depths of your genius. I am here to support you on this journey, offering guidance as you navigate the challenges and celebrate victories. By understanding and applying the lessons shared, you will not only achieve personal fulfillment but also make a meaningful impact on the world. You came to make a huge impact, and this is your pathway to doing just that.

Here are Some Things for you to Remember as you Explore Your Sensory Superpowers:

You are so Much More Than Your Conscious Mind. While your conscious mind is adept at handling everyday tasks, it is only the tip of the iceberg of your true potential. Deep inside you lies a vast reservoir of intuition, creativity, and innate wisdom. This part of you, known as the subconscious or superconscious mind, is where your sensory superpowers reside. It holds the key to understanding your true self, guiding you through life with purpose and clarity. By connecting with and harnessing this inner power, you can transcend the limitations of conscious thought, access a realm of unlimited possibilities, and transform your life in extraordinary ways. Embrace the fullness of your being, for you are a dynamic, multifaceted individual capable of greatness.

You Have Innate Superpowers: You are so much more than what you think, for you have innate superpowers. The daily thoughts are just one aspect of your mental landscape. Beyond these thoughts lies a realm of innate abilities and intuitive insights, which are your true superpowers. These superpowers—your Clair-senses—allow you to perceive the world in ways that go beyond ordinary thinking. Clairvoyance, Clairaudience, Clairgustance, Clairscent, and Clairsentience are real abilities within you, waiting to be uncovered, recognized, and embraced. By tapping into these superpowers, you can navigate life with greater awareness and understanding, making decisions that honor your true self and enhance your connections with others. Embrace these abilities, for they are a testament to the extraordinary potential that enables you to live a life of profound depth, fulfillment, and success.

You can function in ways that honor you and others. Embracing your unique abilities and understanding your true self allows you to navigate life with integrity and respect. By using your superpowers, you can make decisions that align with your values and foster positive relationships. Functioning in ways that honor yourself means being true to your deepest desires while simultaneously considering the well-being of others. This balanced approach creates a harmonious existence where your actions not only benefit you but also uplift and support others. By integrating your sensory superpowers into your daily life, you cultivate an environment of mutual respect, empathy, and understanding, paving the way for personal growth and collective harmony.

Your journey is just beginning in self-discovery. The path of self-discovery is an ongoing adventure. Every step you take uncovers new layers of your potential, revealing the depths of your true abilities and self. As you embark on this journey, remember that each experience, challenge, and triumph brings you closer to a profound understanding of who you are. This journey is not about reaching a destination but about embracing the ongoing process of growth and exploration. With each discovery, you gain greater clarity and insight into your unique abilities and how they can be used to enrich your life and the lives of those around you. Celebrate the beginnings, the milestones, and the endless possibilities that lie ahead as you continue to uncover the extraordinary facets of your being.

Your superpowers are showing up in many ways. Throughout this journey, you've discovered your innate superpowers—those unique abilities that set you apart and empower you to perceive the world in extraordinary ways.

These have always been within you, subtly guiding your experiences and interactions. Recognizing and identifying these abilities is the first step toward harnessing their full potential. Now, with the insights and tools provided in this book, you have a clear pathway to not only acknowledge but also actively use these superpowers. By embracing and refining your Clair-senses, you can navigate life with greater confidence and clarity, transforming your perceptions and awareness into powerful assets that enhance your everyday experiences and contribute to your personal growth and success.

Everything you have ever wanted to experience in this life is already within you. Often, people seek external validation or search for skills and abilities outside themselves, believing these will fulfill their desires or aspirations. However, the truth is that everything you need is already within you. I have encountered numerous individuals who express a longing to be Clairvoyant, only to realize, through our conversations, that they already possess this ability. Within minutes, they can see how their intuitive insights have been guiding them all along. This realization is a powerful reminder that you are inherently equipped with the capabilities you seek. Your journey is about uncovering and embracing these gifts, rather than acquiring them from external sources. By turning inward and recognizing your latent potential, you can unlock a world of experiences and possibilities that align with your deepest desires and true self. Embrace this inner wealth and let it guide you to a life of fulfillment and purpose.

That whatever you want already wants you. Your desires and aspirations are not mere fantasies; they are reflections of your true potential and inner calling. When you deeply desire something, it is often because you are inherently aligned with that goal or experience. This alignment suggests that what you seek is also seeking you. The universe operates on the principle of resonance, where like attracts like. Your genuine desires are indicators of your path and purpose, drawing you toward the experiences, opportunities, and people that will help you fulfill them. Embrace the idea that your goals and dreams are already within reach, waiting for you to recognize and claim them. By aligning your thoughts, actions, and intentions with what you truly want, you create a magnetic force that brings these desires into your reality. Trust that the universe supports your journey and that your aspirations are not only possible but are actively seeking to manifest in your life.

Coming home to yourself is one of the most beautiful and fulfilling journeys you can undertake. By exploring the things that make you unique and special, you embark on a profound path of self-discovery. Taking a deep dive into the unique aspects of who you are—your innate superpowers, distinctive traits, and personal experiences—you begin to uncover the true essence of your being. This exploration is not just about identifying what sets you apart, but about embracing and celebrating these differences as the core of your individuality. Each step you take in understanding yourself brings you closer to a sense of home within your skin. It is a process of recognizing and appreciating your inherent worth, talents, and potential. By exploring what makes you different and special, you honor your authentic self and create a life that is deeply fulfilling and aligned with your true nature. This journey back to yourself is beautiful, empowering, and ultimately, the most genuine way to live.

You can thrive and have success in every area of life by using your superpowers to build and develop your intuition and discernment. Your innate superpowers—Clairvoyance, Clairaudience, Clairgustance, Clairscent, and Clairsentience—are not just extraordinary abilities; they are practical tools that can significantly benefit your daily life. By harnessing these superpowers, you can sharpen your intuition and improve your discernment, allowing you to make decisions with confidence and clarity. This heightened awareness helps you navigate complex situations, understand others more deeply, and foresee potential outcomes, leading to greater success in your personal and professional endeavors. When you trust and develop your intuitive insights, you align yourself with your true purpose and potential, creating a life that is not only successful but also deeply fulfilling. Embracing your superpowers enables you to thrive, transforming challenges into opportunities and dreams into reality.

You can make decisions confidently, without questioning yourself or fearing the impact on others. By developing and trusting your innate superpowers, you gain the confidence to make decisions that align with your true self and highest good. This newfound clarity allows you to act decisively and authentically, free from the paralyzing effects of self-doubt and second-guessing. You no longer need to worry excessively about the reactions or feelings of others, as your decisions come from a place of integrity and mutual respect. When you trust your intuition and inner guidance, you create outcomes that honor both your needs and the well-being of those around you. This balance fosters harmony in your relationships and interactions, enabling you to navigate life's complexities with grace and assurance. Embrace this empowered state of being, where your decisions reflect your true essence and contribute positively to the world.

Miracles await you in your personal transformation. This book was crafted with your success in mind across all areas of life. As you embark on this journey of self-discovery and empowerment, know that extraordinary transformations and miracles are within your reach. This book was written to guide and support you in unlocking your fullest potential. By embracing your innate superpowers and harnessing your intuitive abilities, you open the door to profound changes in every aspect of your life. Whether it's your career, relationships, health, or personal growth, the insights and practices shared in these pages are designed to propel you towards remarkable achievements and fulfillment. Trust in the process and believe in the miracles that await you. Your transformation will not only catapult your success but also inspire those around you, creating a ripple effect of positive change and empowerment.

Knowing oneself is the pathway to excellence. Self-knowledge is the cornerstone of true excellence. When you have a deep understanding of who you are, your strengths, and your unique abilities, you can navigate life with a clear sense of direction and purpose. This inner clarity allows you to make decisions that are aligned with your true self, fostering a sense of authenticity and integrity in everything you do. By knowing yourself, you can leverage your innate talents and superpowers to overcome challenges, seize opportunities, and achieve your goals with confidence. This journey of self-discovery leads to a profound mastery of your potential, enabling you to excel in all areas of life. Embrace the path of self-knowledge, for it is through understanding and honoring your true self that you unlock the doors to greatness and achieve lasting success.

By incorporating a few simple practices into your daily routine, you can significantly enhance your Clair-senses and deepen your intuitive abilities.

Daily Mindfulness Exercises: Practice being present and aware of your sensory insights and information. Take moments throughout the day to focus on what you see, hear, taste, smell, and feel. This heightened awareness helps you connect more deeply with your environment and enhances your sensory perceptions.

Journaling Prompts: Reflect on your daily experiences with your Clair-senses. Write what you perceive and how it influences your interactions and decisions. Journaling not only helps you track your progress but also allows you to gain insights into how your intuitive abilities are developing.

Sensory Awareness Activities: Engage in activities that help you gain even more awareness of your Clair-senses, such as meditation, nature walks, and artistic expression. These activities foster a deeper connection with your inner self and the world around you, further developing your intuitive skills.

Pay attention to others: Start paying attention to what information you gain about others and practice using your art of communication with them once their superpower is defined.

Use your superpowers as discernment: Your ability to "read" what is seen and unseen is the best way to gauge what decisions you make in life, based on the intel you received through your specific superpower. This can guide you home to knowing the highest good for yourself and others and assist in making choices based on your inner guidance system that shows you the information you need to make informed decisions with ease.

Sharing is caring: The more you share what you are learning with others, the more you validate what you've learned and can help others glean from your expertise.

By dedicating time to these practices, you can develop and strengthen your Clairsenses, transforming them into powerful tools for navigating your life. After writing my first book, The Inmate and the Medium, I was informed by a PR firm that six months of focused study can make you an expert in any field. By applying this principle to your Clair-senses, you will find yourself becoming more attuned to your intuitive superpowers, leading to greater clarity, confidence, and success in all areas of your life.

As you deepen your mastery of your Clair-senses, you will come to realize that true greatness lies not only in exceptional talents but also in the unique combination of abilities that each of us possesses. While the concept of genius is often associated with prodigies and extraordinary talents, it is much more inclusive and accessible. You may have thought of a genius as someone exceptionally intelligent; however, in the context of this journey, greatness encompasses the unique blend of your innate abilities that allows you to perceive, interpret, and influence the world in impactful ways. By embracing this deeper definition, you recognize that you already possess these qualities within. Instead of seeking validation or power from external sources, you can own your unique abilities by acknowledging and harnessing your sensory superpowers. This self-empowerment means trusting your intuition, honoring your unique talents, and confidently navigating your path. By embracing your true potential, you step into a life of purpose and fulfillment, making informed decisions and creating meaningful achievements. You are the architect of your destiny, and your unique abilities are the key to unlocking your greatest accomplishments.

True genius lies within the unique constellation of your sensory superpowers—Clairvoyance, Clairaudience, Clairgustance, Clairscent, and Clairsentience. These abilities enable you to interact with the world on a deeper level, offering you perspectives and insights that go beyond ordinary perception. By recognizing and harnessing these abilities, you can tap into a wellspring of intuitive knowledge and creativity that guides you in making profound contributions to your life and the lives of others.

Harnessing your sensory superpowers is about more than just personal enhancement; it's about using these superpowers to live a life with purpose and influence. When you embrace your genius, you align your actions with your deepest values and highest desires. This alignment empowers you to make decisions with clarity and confidence, create meaningful connections, and inspire those around you. Your unique abilities become a force for positive change, helping you to navigate challenges, seize opportunities, and leave a lasting impact on the world.

As you continue this journey of self-discovery, remember that your genius is not a fixed trait but a dynamic and evolving aspect of who you are. By continuously exploring and developing your sensory superpowers, you expand your capacity for innovation, empathy, and leadership. This book serves as a guide to help you unlock and cultivate your genius, providing you with the tools and insights needed to transform your life and achieve your fullest potential.

Historical figures like Helen Keller and Ludwig van Beethoven exemplify how deeply understanding and utilizing one's sensory abilities can lead to extraordinary achievements. Keller and Beethoven are great examples of owning the genius within by using their senses in extraordinary ways which allowed them to overcome severe disabilities and leave indelible impact in the world.

Helen Keller, despite being both deaf and blind, learned to communicate through her heightened sense of touch. Her ability to perceive the world through feeling enabled her to connect deeply with her surroundings and with others, leading to her becoming a renowned author, lecturer, and advocate for people with disabilities. Keller's story is a testament to the power of self-knowledge and the extraordinary potential that lies within each of us. Her life demonstrates that by understanding and embracing our unique abilities, we can transcend perceived limitations and make significant contributions to the world.

Ludwig van Beethoven, one of the greatest composers in history, continued to create masterpieces even after losing his hearing. Beethoven's profound inner clear-hearing sense allowed him to 'hear' the music within his mind, leading to the composition of some of his most celebrated works during his later years. His inner resilience and ability to rely on his sensory superpowers exemplify how embracing one's unique capabilities can lead to exceptional achievements, despite external challenges.

By embracing your sensory superpowers, you too can transcend limitations and be a beacon of innovation and inspiration. Just as Keller and Beethoven harnessed their abilities to overcome their challenges and achieve greatness, you can tap into your intuitive senses to navigate life's obstacles and realize your full potential. This journey of self-discovery and mastery empowers you to break free from conventional constraints and create a life of purpose and impact.

When you fully understand and utilize your sensory superpowers, you become a source of inspiration for others. Your journey of self-knowledge not only transforms your own life but also serves as a guiding light for those around you. By leading through example, you encourage others to explore their unique abilities and pursue their paths to excellence. Embrace your sensory superpowers and let them illuminate the way to a future where you can make a lasting, positive difference in the world.

True leadership is characterized by self-awareness and the ability to guide others toward their potential. By mastering your sensory superpowers—Clairvoyance, Clairaudience,

Clairgustance, Clairscent, and Clairsentience—you gain a profound understanding of your unique strengths and how to leverage them in ways beyond comprehension. This self-mastery not only enhances your personal and professional life but also enables you to inspire and support others in discovering their abilities.

As you become more attuned to your sensory superpowers, your decision-making process becomes more intuitive and informed. This heightened awareness allows you to foresee potential outcomes and navigate complex situations with confidence. Your ability to anticipate and respond to challenges with clarity and insight sets you apart as a leader who is proactive, and adaptive and is a huge asset in the workplace.

Having a deep empathy is a hallmark of effective leadership. By developing your Clair-senses, you enhance your capacity to connect with others on a deeper level, understanding their needs, emotions, and perspectives. This empathetic approach fosters trust and collaboration, creating a supportive environment where everyone feels valued and heard. Your ability to empathize deeply will be noticed and respected by those around you, strengthening your influence and impact.

As your skills and awareness grow, so does your impact. Your presence becomes a force for positive change, inspiring others to pursue their journeys of self-discovery and mastery. By embodying the principles of authenticity, integrity, and compassion, you lead by example, encouraging others to explore their potential and contribute meaningfully to their communities and fields.

Leadership is not just about personal achievement; it's about contributing to the greater good. By harnessing your sensory superpowers, you become a catalyst for positive change, driving innovation and progress. Your ability to see beyond the ordinary, hear the unspoken, and feel the subtle energies of the world positions you as a visionary leader who can guide others toward a brighter future.

Embrace your role as a leader and let your mastery of your Clair-senses illuminate the way for others. Your journey of self-discovery and empowerment will not only transform your own life but also inspire and uplift those around you, creating a ripple effect of positive change and growth.

Let me share a few stories of individuals who have successfully applied the principles discussed in this book:

- Shaun: By developing his Clairvoyance, Shaun was able to foresee potential business challenges and navigate his company to new heights of success by recognizing that he sees things others in the meetings do not. He began to speak up and contribute in ways he never thought of before. He went from feeling unnoticed to receiving kudos and recognition for his contributions. Now he is asked to give insights into problem solving.

- Malena: Utilizing Clairaudience, Malena connected with her inner voice, which guided her through significant life changes with confidence and clarity. Her relationships with her mom and family improved and her acceptance of what she hears brought her profound insight into what was hidden from others. She was able to use this to heal herself and others.

- Janet: One day after a huge breakthrough, her Clairgustance awakened, and her enjoyment of food was enhanced. She began to see how much she loved food, and how much it meant to her, and now has monthly meetings where she invites people to taste the culinary experiences she prepares while connecting with others. (I've eaten her food, and it is delicious!)

- Auti: She began to realize that the field she was most drawn to was skin care products, lotions, moisturizers, and other delicate smells. The more inner work she does, the more heightened her ability to smell what product to share with her clients. This has helped her to make sales and expand her business in intuitive ways.

- Maria: Was plagued with being a Clairsentient. She felt burdened and heavy with the feelings of others and her translation of what they were going through. With loving guidance and through consistent practice of Clairsentience wisely, Maria found that her empathy and understanding of others deepened, without taking on their energy. She became a witness instead, transforming her relationships at work and home into healthy ones. She is freer without carrying the energy of others.

By embracing your sensory superpowers and the genius within, you create a world of possibilities. You can live a life characterized by limitless potential. As we close this book, remember that each day is a new opportunity to apply the lessons learned and continue your journey of exploration and transformation.

To further your exploration of mastering your sensory superpowers and to connect with others who share your interests globally, refer to the Free Resources page to find out how you can be supported further.

Thank you for allowing me to guide you through this transformative process. May the path you choose be illuminated by the knowledge you have gained and the genius you have embraced. Own your genius, and let it shine forth in every aspect of your life.

I would love to hear about your journey and how this book has impacted you through the free Private Global Community. Please share your stories and experiences through reviews, social media, or directly contact me. Your feedback is invaluable and helps shape future projects.

ACKNOWLEDGEMENT

To my beautiful children, Tyler and Keri who have witnessed their mom create and destroy things in big ways, who unwaveringly loved me unconditionally, who witnessed me doing things you didn't understand, but supported me all along the way. You have been the reason to go on in life, to be where I am, to live in love, and to share with others. You both have succeeded so much in this life and I am so happy that you chose to share this lifetime with me. I love you both so much and thank you for being such a healthy blend of support and challenge. Our relationships and those with your precious families are the light of my life. You mean the world to me and I'm so thankful for you. I love you!!!

My heartfelt thanks go to the thousands of clients who have unknowingly contributed to this book, that I've had the pleasure of working with throughout my life. The insights I gained during your sessions—where you learned about concepts, spiritual and universal laws, and how to define and utilize your superpowers—are the result of a lifetime of study for me. You, dear ones, have been the catalyst for these lessons and the knowledge I've accumulated by researching and studying human behavior and the human experience.

Your abilities and how you've applied them personally and collectively have greatly enriched the content of this book. Thank you for touching my life, enhancing my understanding of my superpowers, and giving me the courage to share what I've gleaned from our journeys together. May you all be blessed by reading this book and gaining an even deeper understanding of yourselves.

To Janet Alexander and Maria Lopez, who bravely invested in your transformations and honored your desire to expand and grow. Your hunger for more has been a catalyst for me. Your unwavering and passionate insistence that more people needed to know about me and what I offer has driven me over the past few years. I wouldn't be here without you, precious ladies!

Your enthusiasm, belief in me, and desire for others to experience the same benefits, miracles, and transformations that you have achieved have been incredible. You have been a driving force in my journey to step out of hiding and do more. Thank you for being the reason I bravely got out of my way and decided to offer more. Your love, devotion, and encouragement have carried me, and I love you both so much!

To all of my previous teachers and coaches...

Steve Harrison: Thank you for being such a catalyst in my life through Quantum Leap. Your programs and wisdom have taught so many how to market and sell our books. Meeting your brother and wife was an added benefit. Thank you for all the private conversations, for putting me on stage, and for allowing me to receive my first standing ovation amongst my peers on your stage. You have encouraged so many of us to grow, expand, and own our genius. Thank you for touching my life.

Jack Canfield: Thank you for inspiring those of us who were new to being authors. I am grateful for the privilege of being in your home twice, experiencing your hospitality, and engaging with others on the cusp of greatness. Your perseverance with the Chicken Soup for the Soul series was and still is an inspiration. I cherish your hugs, our conversations, and your belief in me. You are a driving force for so many who aspire to give and offer more.

Tony Selimi: Thank you for showing me that I could manifest anything I wanted. Your belief in me and your ability to hold space were invaluable. Many days, I stood on your belief in me and learned even more about my ability to be a conscious alchemist. I discovered I could manifest the money to pay you and others who taught me vital life lessons. Thank you for being you; I love you dearly.

Vrinda Normand: Thank you for teaching me so much about marketing and for playing a significant role in my ability to conduct my workshops. You were a catalyst for me, encouraging me to offer more and support my clients as they delved deeper into the knowledge I had to share.

Kathy Motlagh: Thank you for teaching me to calm my mind, manage my time, and recognize that I am the director of my thoughts and dreams. You helped me understand how to make empowered decisions, discern what resonated and what didn't, and have the courage to hire the experts I needed to move forward.

Monique McDonald: My dear speaking coach, thank you for being a loving force in my life. Your belief in me and your wisdom has been instrumental in preparing me for this book and the stage. You helped open my voice and gave me the courage to speak freely and authentically. Thank you for your guidance.

Bill Walsh: Thank you for being a significant part of my growth and expansion. From our first private conversation, you saw something in me and encouraged me to take leaps of faith. Your generosity, drive, and clairvoyant abilities are inspirational. You saw me and others and have been the catalyst for so many who were ready to launch. You have given me opportunities that I've never had before and I will forever be grateful for your wisdom, teachings, tools, and techniques. You have changed my life entirely in just a few months, and I love you for it!

Angel Tuccy: Thank you for showing me that writing a book in 60 days is possible. Your model, poise, and grace have been amazing. I am grateful for your support, encouragement, and the space you held for those of us who bravely said "YES!" You are a beautiful soul, and I am thankful to have met you and worked with you.

Michael Neeley and Krista Inochovsky: Thank you for your encouragement in my launching in a much bigger way. Your generosity of spirit and kindness are evident in all that you do, and I am grateful to call you my friends. Thank you for lending your ears, sharing your wisdom, and helping me discern what works and what doesn't.

To my Older Souls Tribe: Your hunger, desire to grow, and commitment to learning have been incredibly encouraging. You have become my family, and I am thankful for each of you. You bravely invest in your growth, understanding the pain and rewards that come with it. You mean the world to me, and I love you all so much. I no longer feel alone because you are my tribe and you touch me daily and encourage me. Witnessing your transformations and helping you achieve your desires is a joy and an honor. You have inspired me to offer more, write more books, and give more classes.

FREE RESOURCES

A great resource for you to understand your abilities and what your top one is, find out more with the UNCOVER YOUR SENSORY SUPERPOWERS. Take the quiz to Find Out Which Special Sense Guides Your Intuition. Go to: https://www.superpowersunleashed.com/quiz and take yours now and see what your senses have to say.

Book your free 15 Discovery Call to find out how you can elevate your abilities, grow them, and use them for your success in life. I'm happy to support you in life. Go to: https://www.tammydemirza.com and scroll down to JV or Discovery Call.

Free Intuitive Guidance. Join my email list at https://www.tammydemirza.com and ask me any question you most want to know and I'll answer you personally as your Intuitive.

Free Masterclass on Manifesting, please join my email list on my website: https://www.tammydemirza.com and ask for your copy.

I invite you to join our community of like-minded individuals who are also on this journey of self-discovery and mastery. You'll find the QR code on the back of this book. Together, we can share experiences, support each other, and continue to grow.

Social Media where you can get a lot of free content:

YouTube: Tammy De Mirza:
https://www.youtube.com/@TammyDeMirza

Twitter: @tammydirza https://twitter.com/TammyDemirza

Instagram: @tammydemirza_official
https://www.instagram.com/tammydemirza_official/

Facebook: https://www.facebook.com/tdemirza

Facebook Public: https://www.facebook.com/tammydemirzapublic

TikTok: tammydemirza https://www.tiktok.com/@tammydemirza

Google: https://www.tammydemirza.com/

LinkedIn: https://www.linkedin.com/in/tammydemirza/

Don't hesitate to reach out—let's explore the potential of your Clair-senses together!

ABOUT THE AUTHOR
Tammy De Mirza
The Breakthrough Alchemist®

TAMMY DE MIRZA, known globally as The Breakthrough Alchemist®, is a distinguished intuitive, author, and spiritual guide dedicated to transforming lives. Her exceptional ability to tap into the conscious, subconscious, and superconscious realms, allows her to unveil hidden barriers that prevent individuals from reaching their fullest potential. Tammy's unique blend of expertise as a mindset coach and transformative guide has touched countless lives, leading them to release limiting beliefs and embrace a life of abundance and fulfillment.

Her journey is one of profound transformation, rising from personal adversities to becoming a beacon of hope and empowerment for many. Tammy's compassionate approach and deep understanding of human potential have earned her a reputation as a trusted mentor and healer. She offers a range of transformative services, including one-on-one sessions, immersive retreats, Life & Breakthrough Transformations in groups and private settings, as well as dynamic live events, which are all designed to foster personal growth and self-realization.

As an author, Tammy has penned two insightful books, 'The Inmate and the Medium' and '65 Signs That You're an Older Soul.' Her writings reflect her deep insights and experiences, providing readers with practical guidance and spiritual wisdom. In her latest book, 'SUPERPOWERS UNLEASHED: Identify and Monetize Your Senses,' Tammy delves into the world of intuitive abilities, guiding readers to harness their innate senses for personal and professional success.

Tammy's expertise extends beyond her writings. She is a sought-after international speaker, featured on numerous TV shows, documentaries, podcasts, and media platforms worldwide. Her engaging presence and powerful messages have inspired audiences globally, offering them the tools and insights needed to achieve their breakthroughs.

Her brand, The Breakthrough Alchemist®, embodies her mission to empower individuals to uncover their inner brilliance and achieve extraordinary transformations. Through her programs, such as the 'Breakthrough Manifestation Formula,' 'Awaken Your Superpowers,' and

'The Power to Choose,' Tammy equips spiritual seekers with the knowledge and skills to navigate their journey towards self-realization and miracles.

Tammy's personal story of overcoming challenges and embracing her true potential serves as a testament to the power of inner transformation. She believes in the importance of self-awareness, understanding personal sensory superpowers, and applying them in relationships and professional settings for success in all areas. Her work emphasizes that with the right guidance and tools, anyone can achieve remarkable success and fulfillment in their lives.

To get the Awakening your Superpowers six-hour course and a day with Tammy as your intuitive to identify your top three superpowers and how you use them, sign up now at: https://www.superpowersunleashed.com

For more information on Tammy's transformative services, books, and upcoming events, visit https://www.tammydemirza.com.

Made in the USA
Columbia, SC
12 September 2024